Jeff F

MW00616950

- Butler lines of 10 serats.
- TRAWcewtal Melitiuu.
" Ayurvedic Momory. Com

THE POWER
OF GOD...
TODAY

by CHRISTINE M. BLAKE

THE POWER OF GOD…TODAY
by Christine M. Blake
www.theblessedreasontrip.com

Published by E. Blake
blessedreasontrip@gmail.com

*Scripture quotations are from the New Revised Standard Version Bible: Catholic Edition, copyright © 1989, 1993 National Council of the Churches of Christ in the United States of America. Used by permission. All rights reserved worldwide.

ISBN (paperback)-13: 978-1-7355332-9-2
ISBN (hardcover)-13: 978-1-7355332-8-5

PRINTED IN THE UNITED STATES OF AMERICA

———

Medical Disclaimer: This book is not intended as a substitute for the medical advice of physicians. The reader should regularly consult a physician in matters relating to his/her health and particularly with respect to any symptoms that may require diagnosis or medical attention.

Disclaimer: This book contains actual events in the author's life. The events, places, people, and conversations listed in this book are factual. When necessary, the names and identifying characteristics of individuals have been changed to maintain anonymity.

———

Cover design by Emily Blake
Cover Illustration Copyright © 2020
Editing by Kimberly (Kim) R. Smith
Author's photography by Emily Blake

Thank you to the all the holy angels and saints
who intercede daily on our behalf...

To the love that binds us all as one –
the love of Christ,
& to the couple who helped me discover it –
Dr. Issam & Kathy Nemeh

contents

preface

THIS BOOK IS NOT meant to be about my own life; it is intended to have a greater purpose. Its main emphasis is God, His wondrous ways, and how He calls each one of us to turn our gaze upon Him.

God is moving in ways most never believed were possible. The miracles sprinkled throughout this book open our minds to the Power of our God and to the reasons why they are occurring, which is to capture our attention, now more than ever.

Last year, a man with a very deep faith prayed over me and everything changed. This one man's prayer created a shift in me so great that every piece of who I am, and how I live, was changed *forever*. This transformation opened my eyes to the sole purpose of my whole life, which is to live for God and for others. It didn't take long for God to whisper into my heart, inviting me to share this truth and calling to help inspire others to seek God's healing and mission in their own lives.

God has encouraged me to write about my life's chain of events and how it has affected the lives of hundreds of others. I have come to understand that with God, *anything* is possible. Jesus is still here walking with us – always caring, listening, and responding to our prayers. God is speaking to us in a variety of ways, one of which is through the people that he places directly in front of us.

I am by no means a special person, and I come from practically nowhere regarding my faith background. I was brought up with a father who is an atheist and a mother who was a serious alcoholic. Mysteriously, I have somehow always known that there is a God and believed deep down the same fundamental beliefs of most Christians.

Since I was a young girl, I felt an invitation to come to know and follow the Lord, even with an upbringing such as mine. I cannot explain the spiritual calling I had written on my heart; all I know is I have always felt it. Sadly, I haven't always followed. There were many years in my life where I was simply going through the motions of existence and sleepwalking my way through my days…my years…my life.

My life was messy and complicated when I was younger. I made numerous mistakes while running from the emotional pain I still carried around from my childhood. I began motherhood at quite an early age, and before I knew it, I was an adult raising three beautiful children. Thankfully, for the most part, once I became a mother, my life began to change. Becoming a mom triggered something inside of me that made me look at life, and all that surrounded me, differently.

A few years later, I escaped a detrimental relationship with my three children. There were, nonetheless, many more trials that we would still have to endure in the upcoming years. Mercifully, God put an angel of a man in our lives to care for us while helping to steer the four of us towards a new and bright beginning. This man was a caring soul, and by the grace of God, came to love me and my three kids, while also promising to take care of us for the rest of his life.

This gentleman's name is Randy. He comes from a Catholic family and upbringing, and so I too became Catholic. We began our lives together with a blessed and traditional Catholic wedding. I had much to learn, but little by little, I became more educated about my new faith. In doing so, I fell in love with it. Randy had no idea that not only was he giving me and my children a new picture of what love truly was, but he was also giving us one of the holiest gifts he could give, the gift of faith. This is what helped me piece together the meaning of my life. Having a more solid belief system in God gave purpose to my life, provided me with a hope for an everlasting happiness, and helped me to endure some of my toughest heartbreaks that were yet to come in my life.

When I married Randy twenty-two years ago, my life finally began going in a positive direction for me and my three children – Collette, Josh, and Matt. Randy adopted the children and took them in as if they were his own. He was an incredible role model for all of them, but perhaps, even more so for my two sons, who needed a male figure to look up to in their life.

Two years after we married, we had a sweet baby girl together. Our daughter's name is Emily and she instantly became my little sidekick since the day she came into this world. Our connection with each other has always been deeper than the typical parent-child, mother-daughter relationship. It is more spiritual in nature. The events that have taken place in our lives in the last year made our special bond grow even deeper.

These past twelve months, God has graciously blessed my daughter and me by calling us on a new journey together. During this time we have helped to bring healing to people who were once strangers, but now through this ministry, they have become some of our most beloved friends. The joys that have come through witnessing healing miracles in others and in our newfound friends have caused my heart to spill over with delight and appreciation. God has opened my eyes, mind, and heart to His many blessings and love that surround me, and all of us, every day.

I have come to recognize that there genuinely is a reason for everything that takes place within our lives. Even the smallest incidents that happen to us have significant meaning if we allow ourselves to see them. Our Lord is in each minute, breath, and invisible detail around us.

The truth most of us already know is that miracles do exist although they occur at rates more numerous than nearly anyone would ever dare to dream. There is plenty of evidence for this all around us if we choose to look. I have seen them, time after time, happen right in front of me. Some miracles I have *seen* and even *felt* take place within my very own body. We must be brave in today's secular world by speaking up to share what God is showing us with these miracles. This way, others can learn about them and may also come to believe.

I prayerfully hope this book can help someone on their path to a deeper faith. One person's journey in life holds more meaning and potential in God's eyes than we could possibly imagine. God is present with us, stepping into our lives, which goes to show just how much He truly loves us. He so much desires a relationship with us that He willingly proves it by walking among us and healing many in the form of miracles, in order to grab our attention and enlighten our minds to this fact.

In the times we live in, it is crucial for people to learn about God's true presence and His universal message for all of us. Sometimes this happens through simple testimonies, which help strengthen and renew our faith, while drawing people closer to God.

Proverbs 27: 17 (NRSV)

Iron sharpens iron,

and one person sharpens the wits of another.

one.

Introduction to Miracles

I WAS FIRST INTRODUCED to the reality of miracles taking place in 2011 when I stumbled onto *The Dr. Oz Show* as I was changing channels on the television. I had been recently diagnosed with a dangerous heart rhythm, to which there were discussions of heart ablation surgery as well as a possible pacemaker. I was intrigued by what I saw on television that one fateful day.

Dr. Oz introduced a medical doctor named Dr. Issam Nemeh. He is a trained doctor with specialties in anesthesiology and general surgery who thousands look to for healing through prayer. There were many people in the audience saying they were healed simply by Dr. Nemeh extending his two hands over them while praying to God. I was fascinated how the patients presented their individual healings and that there was scientific evidence proving their miracle stories.

Later that same day, my interest grew as I spent hours researching this doctor who resided in Ohio. I learned a great deal about him online, and much to my surprise, I discovered there was a book written about him as well. The book is titled *Miracles Every Day,* written by Maura Poston Zagrans, who followed Dr. Nemeh and his wife Kathy for nearly two years in their healing ministry and at his office. The whole concept of healing was so inspiring to me that I ordered the book without hesitation.

When the book came in the mail, I read it from beginning to end all in one sitting. I could not put it down. Everything I read gave me such cause for hope that healing through the intercession of one man's prayers could be so powerful. There were many miraculous accounts from people telling what had happened after receiving a prayer from this doctor at his office or from a healing service. The book also described how both the doctor and his wife had Jesus, Mary, angels, and even saints stepping into their lives on a daily basis. I treasured the story about Dr. Nemeh, and even though I had some major health issues going on at the time, I had become distracted with my everyday life of being a wife and mother of four children, while running a business from home. So at the time, I didn't do much with what I had learned until a few months later when a moment of desperation took hold of me.

It all began one evening in May of 2011, as I was tucking my youngest of four into bed. I was speaking with my daughter who was 11 years old at the time, about her day, rubbing her stomach as we talked, and noticed something irregular. My hand slid across her right ribcage and came across a bump. This knot felt hard like a bone. I knew it didn't feel right, nor did it appear to be a natural part of her ribs. I quickly checked Emily's left side, and once I discovered it was only located on her right side, I felt a flame of fear ignite inside me. I didn't want her to see my worry, so I hurriedly kissed her goodnight, but before leaving her room, I asked her if this bump caused her any pain. She was startled by my question, saying she never even noticed it being there before. I left her room, consumed by a dizzying spell of worries, which led to a sleepless night for both me and my husband.

The next morning, we whisked Emily into the doctor's office to be scheduled for CT scans and an MRI. They informed us that this growth was indeed a tumor. They couldn't be positive, but they were pretty sure it was benign at the time. However, they told us due to its location, there were risks of it leading to cancer at some point in her upcoming years. Her future was uncertain and only time would tell what was to come. My worries and anxieties led me to take a second look at Dr. Nemeh and his healing ministry. I decided I would do whatever I could to have Emily go in front of him for a prayer.

In the days ahead, I went back online and found that Dr. Nemeh had a healing service coming up near Chicago in July 2011. I was astounded and beyond grateful when I discovered there were openings left, and that it was close enough for us to attend. It would be nearly five hours of driving, but I remember thinking, *five hours is nothing if there is a possibility of a miracle.* I immediately purchased three tickets – one for my daughter Emily, one for my husband Randy, and one for myself. Then, we waited two months for the special day, which provided us with a remarkable gift of hope.

In the time between May and July, I began to inform Emily and Randy about the miraculous stories I had read in the book about Dr. Nemeh. My husband was skeptical and wasn't all that excited about attending a healing service, but considering our fears with Emily, he was willing to come for her sake. Emily was young, but she was already very much in tune with the power of God. When the morning came for us to go, Emily and I were both excited and nervous all at the same time.

Since we had a five-hour drive to Chicago, we left early in the morning to ensure we would be on time. When we arrived at the hotel where the service was to be held, we noticed we had an hour or two to spare. So while Randy was walking around looking at items in the entryway, Emily and I decided to grab a high-top table and sit near the lobby. The seats we sat in stood facing the entryway and large picture windows that overlooked the front of the hotel, while our backs were turned to those walking around in the lobby. As we were engaged in our conversation about our expectations for the day, a most profound incident took place, which still makes me smile when I think about it to this day.

While we were chatting, something suddenly grabbed our attention, causing us to immediately stop talking and sit completely still. It took us both by surprise, because a most unusual feeling came over each of us at the same time. This experience felt like an incredible wave of spiritual perception as it went in one sweeping motion, from our heads down to our toes. As soon as we looked at each other in awe, Emily and I realized we had both had the same amazing encounter. We were speechless because it was unlike anything we had ever felt before.

We soon realized that this incredible feeling was caused by someone walking behind us. We each felt this person's overwhelming presence, which we knew was holy in nature. As we followed this tugging in our hearts, we both turned around and fixed our eyes on one man. We discovered that it was Dr. Issam Nemeh. He was continuing to make his way down a nearby hall. As we stared at him, Dr. Nemeh looked towards us with a most loving, joyful gaze, which my daughter and I felt internally and spiritually. During this indescribable moment, I believe we truly felt Christ's presence coming from within Dr. Nemeh.

I have never discussed this moment we experienced with Dr. Nemeh, as he is a most humble man, who says he is only doing God's will for his life. Nevertheless, I do feel I must share this information, as it may help others appreciate Dr. Nemeh's tangible love and bond with Christ.

As Emily and I shared what we both felt with each other, we could hardly believe what had happened. This incident made us become more excited than ever about the healing service. The event was about to begin, so the three of us started walking towards the conference room where the healing service was to be held.

In the hallway outside the room, there was a long table to check in with a few volunteers standing nearby to scan our tickets. There was no paperwork or any questionnaires to fill out beforehand. To the side of the table was the doctor's wife, Kathy Nemeh. She greeted us with an incredibly warm welcome. She had a beautiful presence about her that instantly made an impression on me. I felt an immediate connection to her, as if I had known her forever.

It was another beautiful moment, which took me by surprise because I had never felt such a strong bond with someone I had just met for the first time. I didn't dwell on it, but it was a peculiar greeting that I distinctly remember. Afterwards, we made our way into the conference room to attend the service.

Once inside, I realized how this whole idea of a healing service seemed absolutely foreign to me. There were at least one hundred people in attendance, and I wondered how many of them thought the same way. The chairs for the healing service were set out in a theater style, all pointed towards the front of the room. The holy and prayerful atmosphere began to stir my spirit. I could tell it was going to be a profound and moving experience before it began.

Kathy introduced her husband and asked everyone to come up for their individual prayer with faith, hope, and courage. Dr. Nemeh then proceeded to give a brief inspirational talk about faith and suggested that we simply surrender and let God, "The Healer," work within us. Soon after, the volunteers began selecting groups of ten people to come to the front of the room for a prayer. All ten of the individuals would stand comfortably side-by-side, and spread out across the front of the room, which allowed some privacy between each person.

Dr. Nemeh approached each person individually and prayed quietly calling on the Holy Spirit through Jesus' name. Watching him pray over others was mesmerizing, as each time his hands were spiritually guided to the area needing healing. He exhibited such a humility and kindness that appeared to radiate right through him. There were no microphones being used, no speaking in tongues, or anything that may have seemed unusual. Instead, it was a very natural, calm scene. The only thing that I was not accustomed to was seeing people falling in the Holy Spirit, but when they did, they had volunteers serve as "catchers" to gently lay people onto the floor.

This did not carry any resemblance to the off-putting scenes I had seen in the past where evangelists seemed to show off by pushing on a participant's forehead and forcefully hollering, "You are healed!" No. What I watched play out in front of me was not like that whatsoever; it actually seemed to be quite the opposite. This prayer service was respectful, quiet, and in one word, *beautiful.*

Dr. Nemeh was impressive to watch. He had a sense of stillness and patience as he went from person to person to pray. The only one who held his attention was the individual standing in front of him during the prayer. The doctor was constantly focused on the spiritual connection taking place between himself, the person being prayed over, and the Holy Spirit. The whole process was stunning to me!

As fascinating as it was, seeing people fall in the Spirit was so unfamiliar to me that I doubted what I was seeing. I began to wonder, *are these people acting? Is this even real?* I couldn't believe how easily my thinking switched, especially after everything I had read about the miracle stories surrounding Dr. Nemeh, and what I had *felt* before the service when Dr. Nemeh walked behind me.

Randy, Emily, and I were in one of the first groups to be called up for a prayer since children and their families are typically chosen first by the volunteers. As Dr. Nemeh walked up to the stranger that stood on my right, I once again *felt* God's presence. As I watched him pray, the person next to me began to fall back. She glided right into the arms of the volunteer. Dr. Nemeh stepped towards me and my heart started racing like never before. I knew it didn't feel like the usual rhythm issues causing my heart rate to increase; no, this time it was God Himself. He had already begun working on my heart before the doctor reached me.

As Dr. Nemeh continued to walk over to me, I felt an incredible intense heat on my heart. My heart rate continued to climb higher and higher, faster and faster, almost to an alarming pace. My concern took my focus off watching the doctor. Then, all at once, I too fell in the Holy Spirit, resting into the arms of a trained volunteer. It happened so fast. I never saw Dr. Nemeh fully reach me or extend his hands in prayer over me, which I later learned from Emily and Randy he most certainly did.

When my eyes reopened, I noticed I was lying on the floor. I still felt the power of the Holy Spirit over me, similar to the feeling of a weighted blanket. I tried to lift my head, but I felt cemented to the floor, as if God wasn't finished with me yet. I began looking around and as I turned to my gaze to the left, I was surprised to discover Emily was also lying on the floor next to me. Her eyes were likewise open, but they were transfixed on her dad. He was in the midst of receiving his prayer from the doctor.

Randy struggled to stay standing. His right knee tried to give and buckle down as Dr. Nemeh prayed, but Randy fought the Holy Spirit trying to embrace him. He caught himself starting to fall back and stood right back up. Following this small dance of Randy's to stay in complete control over his body, Dr. Nemeh continued praying and his hands hovered over Randy's heart. I couldn't help but wonder what he was praying for exactly. Sadly, Randy never fully allowed himself to surrender. He swayed a bit more here and there but remained standing the entire time. After his prayer was finished and Dr. Nemeh had moved on, I noticed Randy seemed out of sorts. It was as if he didn't know how to react. Looking lost in his own thoughts, he went straight back to his original seat.

It took Emily and me a few more minutes before we were able to stand back up and head back to our seats. It is challenging to describe what I experienced when resting in the Spirit, except to say I had an incredible amount of peace wash over me that came straight from Heaven. There is *nothing* else like it.

As the three of us sat in our seats, we decided to stay only a little while longer at the service. After watching a few more strangers go up for prayer, my husband was ready to leave. I was sad, but I didn't argue, as I was grateful for the fact we were able to come in the first place. Had it been up to me, we would have stayed there all day to watch what God had in store for others!

As the three of us got back into our car to return home, Emily and I were both immensely moved by our experience. We wondered what had happened during the prayers and how amazing it was to rest in the Holy Spirit. I would have never thought that resting in the Spirit would have happened to me. It left me trying to understand how that happened, not only to me, but also to Emily. Randy didn't seem as impressed, and since we were not all on the same page, we stopped talking about it on our drive back to Iowa.

After returning home, we told our three older children – Collette, Josh, and Matt, as well as my in-laws, about our experiences. Even though we didn't understand much of it at the time, we would later learn our prayer with Dr. Nemeh would leave a long-lasting effect on us. For several months, I would lie awake at night replaying the healing service in my mind. I never forgot about it, even though it took many years before I recognized, pieced together, and fully understood what had undeniably happened there that day.

Emily had many appointments with doctors and specialists throughout the years, along with periodic CT scans to keep an eye on things. I am beyond grateful to report the tumor stayed benign, and although it grew a little bit in size as she continued to grow, that was the extent of her issues.

Several months after the healing service, I went back to my cardiologist for a "checkup." Test results indicated I had no signs of heart rhythm troubles, specifically ventricular tachycardia (V-tach), which was my original diagnosis. My cardiologist was puzzled and referred me to another specialist, an electrophysiologist at the University of Iowa, for further testing. Many more tests and appointments later, my doctors were never able to find an abnormal heart rhythm issue again. Eventually, they reported that I must have been "misdiagnosed."

I was thrilled to learn that heart surgery was off the table, and all my initial fears ceased. However, it saddens me to think that I never connected the dots between the prayer at the healing service and the doctors calling it a "misdiagnosis." I had taken their newfound words as pure fact, and I never put it together that I had experienced a healing…until eight years later.

Mark 8:17-18 (NRSV)
"Do you still not perceive or understand? Are your hearts hardened?
Do you have eyes, and fail to see?
Do you have ears, and fail to hear?
And do you not remember?"

two.

God's Wake-up Call

GOD DECIDED HE WAS going to get my attention for good this time. In May 2014, after many years of going from doctor to doctor trying to figure out what was wrong, I was officially diagnosed by a rheumatologist with an autoimmune disease, systemic lupus. Lupus is characterized by a kind of allergic reaction by the body, in which the immune system sees the body's own healthy tissues and cells as foreign, which often leads the body to attack itself. It is a chronic disease, meaning that anyone who develops lupus will have it for the rest of his or her life. Since lupus is a serious disease, I sought a second opinion at the Mayo Clinic in Rochester, Minnesota in April 2016. The physician there agreed with the original diagnosis and treatment.

Even though I had struggled with flare-ups and rigorous lupus symptoms, such as fluid around my heart and failing digestive organs, for years, more serious medical problems began to surface in late 2018. It was an extremely agonizing phase in my life. I felt on occasion, that I was more of a nuisance to my family because of my illness, symptoms, and pain. Most of the time, I felt exhausted, sick, achy, and often I couldn't function very well in my normal day-to-day activities.

I was originally prescribed a medication to stop my body from attacking itself and to protect my organs, with the goal being to help me live a long and healthy life. However, in December of 2018, this same medication that was intended to improve my health was now the source of several negative side effects. Nearly two years after beginning the regimen, a doctor realized I was improperly dosed, prescribed almost twice the normal amount for my body weight.

This medication, even properly dosed, already carried many health risks and side effects. One of the potential threats is color blindness, which could eventually develop into a complete loss of vision, causing irreversible cell damage, even if you stopped taking the drug itself. Toxins tend to build up in the bloodstream from taking the medication, leading to a specific toxicity that causes blindness. The warning signs I was experiencing indicated that this was what was happening to me.

My daughter Emily was the first to notice that I was having symptoms of colorblindness. I made an appointment with my ophthalmologist and he concurred with testing that there was an alarming degree of change taking place. He forwarded his findings to my rheumatologist, who felt it was too risky to take me off the medication. If I were to stop, the next step up would be to take a more potent drug that carried even heavier risks. So, in the larger scheme of things, losing my sight, or at the very least, being unable to differentiate colors, was a small price to pay in comparison.

In all honesty, even though this drug was helping to save my life, I was still concerned about the possibility of losing my eyesight down the road. Therefore, I scheduled another appointment with the Mayo Clinic to get a second opinion on how to best move forward. The appointment was scheduled for February 2019.

One night, in late December of 2018, as things began to deteriorate even further for me, Emily recommended, "Why don't you try to make a medical appointment to see Dr. Nemeh?"

I hadn't thought about Dr. Nemeh in some time and was taken back by her suggestion. Unfortunately, I still hadn't figured out what had *really* happened with my heart when I first received a prayer at the 2011 healing service. After Emily's suggestion, I did remember reading that Dr. Nemeh had a medical office in Westlake, Ohio and treated patients there. Emily reminded me that over the previous summer, she had randomly picked up the same book I read about Dr. Nemeh so long ago, *Miracles Every Day*. I had kept the book on a shelf in our living room all these years. One day, on a whim, she picked it up and read it for the first time. Now we realize this was nothing short of a God-inspired moment.

A few days later, when I was at work, employed as a faith formation coordinator for a Catholic church, I decided to call Dr. Nemeh's Ohio office. I was surprised when Kathy Nemeh, the doctor's wife, answered the office phone herself. I was instantly brought back to the first time I had met her, as if it had happened yesterday. I remembered how I felt like I had known her forever, as if she was family. I smiled, and even chuckled under my breath at how curious that connection to her was.

I explained to Kathy I was calling to make an appointment to visit the doctor. She asked what was going on with me and I gave as many details possible. She quickly assured me that her husband treats many people in similar situations on a regular basis. They had a cancellation a few weeks out and she inquired if that would work for me. I was thrilled at the timing being so soon and told her that I would take it and do whatever I could to make it work.

Kathy stated that my appointment would be on a Friday night at 9:45 p.m. I couldn't believe what I was hearing. I knew Dr. Nemeh worked long hours from what I had read in the past, but I guess when I heard her actually provide that late of a time, I was a bit stunned. Kathy explained he normally makes two appointments with people having similar medical issues, usually spacing them several days apart. However, since I was coming from such a great distance, she would schedule my first appointment on a Friday night and the second one would be the following day, a *Saturday,* right away in the morning.

I don't remember speaking much in reply after hearing such irregular appointment times. I think I was in shock, plus I still couldn't believe that I was really going to be able to see Dr. Nemeh. Kathy went on to tell me there was a healing service that same weekend on Sunday, so if it was possible, I should try to attend that as well before coming back home. Her reference to a healing service reminded me of how I had first felt when Dr. Nemeh walked by behind me and how I fell in the Spirit as he stepped towards me to pray. I was thrilled at the idea of having the opportunity to attend another healing service. I ended up having Kathy schedule me for the two individual office times she had mentioned. The healing service was a separate matter, for which I registered individually online via the website: *www.pathtofaith.com.*

After our conversation, I was at a complete loss for words. I sat quietly for a few moments reflecting on the idea that I would really be going to Ohio to see Dr. Nemeh and Kathy! I took some time to recollect myself and let everything sink in a little before calling my family to tell them about my scheduled appointments with Dr. Nemeh, the same man who had made such a huge impression on both Emily and me eight years before. I was especially excited to call Emily. I could hardly wait to share the wonderful news with her!

I had no doubt that Emily would want to come, as she was the one who had originally come up with the whole idea. The main reason I wanted her there with me was because she had her own medical issues. Emily no longer had trouble from the growth on her rib, but she had been suffering from a painful case of endometriosis for many years. At times, the pain was debilitating for her.

Eventually, Emily's doctor prescribed medication to reduce her pain, control the size, and keep the tissue from spreading. Unfortunately, we weren't initially well-informed on the subject, and at the time, we were told this medication was the only effective treatment. Emily began to struggle with the possible harmful side effects artificial hormones could have on her body, not to mention their ethical and moral implications. She conducted her own investigative work and read numerous studies indicating these hormones were potentially unsafe. We began to understand that Emily could end up being in a similar situation as me if she continued taking her medication. On the other hand, if she stopped taking the artificial hormones, she was concerned that the endometriosis could possibly lead to fertility issues.

Once I told her I had this appointment scheduled with Dr. Nemeh, she insisted on coming along, but not out of any concern for herself. She desired only to be there out of love and support for me. My heart was set on her coming with me because of the amazing opportunity for her to be healed. God placed a longing in her heart at an early age to become a mother and have a family. I knew how much it meant to her, and I wanted to put the possible complications from endometriosis behind her for good.

My three older kids were all grown, independent, and busy with their work, so I knew only Emily would be able to join me, but I hoped maybe my husband would come, too. At first, I thought how great it would be to have Randy there with us, especially to be our pillar of support. I also considered the idea that Randy may be able to surrender more this time at the healing service, but the more I thought about it, the more someone else kept coming to mind. It began to weigh on my heart, causing me to reconsider asking Randy and ask a family friend that I worked with instead. My coworker Nancy was in the process of going through her second round of breast cancer. Her prognosis was decent, but many details were still touch-and-go. Nancy needed a healing too, and I couldn't seem to shake the idea of bringing her with us.

Since Christmas was around the corner, I decided to ask her if she would be willing to come with Emily and me to Ohio. I explained that

I would like to give the trip, including a ticket to the healing service, as a Christmas gift to her out of friendship. I did not expect anything in return, except for her hope in finding a healing. I told her that I understood she had huge expenses with the cancer treatments, medical bills from surgery, plus the normal costs of the holidays, and I asked her to talk it over with her husband. They both agreed to graciously accept my offer to allow her to partake in this trip of a lifetime.

Nancy is a lovely lady inside and out. She is a mother to four beautiful daughters. Admittedly, she was a little reluctant to join us at first, mostly because she had recently had another issue surface. She had a bulging disc in her back, which made it challenging for her to sit still for long periods of time, especially in a vehicle. I decided to help her along with the decision whether to come or not by lending her my copy of the book *Miracles Every Day*. I thought it might help her have a better idea of who Dr. Nemeh is and what exactly he does. It didn't take long before Nancy read the book and fully committed to going with us, despite her worries about traveling in pain.

After inviting Nancy, I recognized it may be somewhat awkward for my husband to join us. I knew the healing Nancy would be searching for was personal in nature, plus having three women traveling in the same car together for over an eight-hour period was maybe more than my husband could handle. I was afraid Randy would be upset that I had invited Nancy. To my surprise, he wasn't upset in the least and thought that her health concerns most definitely warranted me asking her to come with us. He did, however, voice his concern about us traveling such a long distance in the middle of January due to the unpredictable winter weather.

Sure enough, we experienced a mighty blizzard a day before we were to leave and there was another storm to the west of us, ready to blast in our direction any day. My family and friends, including my boss, warned us not to go as it could be treacherous. People from all directions were telling us we shouldn't make the trip. Emily and I both had a strong sense that we were meant to go regardless of the unknowns. We knew and trusted God would watch over us, despite the many people advising us not to go.

We headed out early Friday morning, allowing plenty of time to make it a comfortable drive without feeling like we had to rush. The roads were surprisingly clear, and my friend was a complete godsend in the car. She has the gift of captivating others through fun-filled stories and laughter, which helped us stay alert on the way there. Once we were within an hour of arriving in Westlake, Ohio, we received a phone call that the doctor was running late. Therefore, they needed to push my appointment back. It was now scheduled for 10:45 p.m. I was again amazed at the late hours the doctor kept.

This extra time allowed us to check into the hotel room that the three of us were sharing, as well as grab a rather late supper. Soon after eating, we headed straight to the doctor's office. We pulled into the parking lot at ten o'clock in the evening. We realized we were forty-five minutes early, but since we were so excited, we couldn't think of much else to do with our time. We figured we might as well be there just in case he was done earlier than expected.

The size of the building was smaller than I had pictured in my mind, but once we were inside, I appreciated how the size of this special place was most irrelevant. It was unlike any other medical office I had ever been to in the past. The atmosphere contained a sacred presence, and the whole office radiated with holiness.

We were warmly welcomed by a lady named Jane. She brought me to a back room to fill out the necessary paperwork for my appointment. I noticed she appeared somewhat tired, but it was ten o'clock at night. I could only imagine how long of a day she had already worked. She explained that we were the doctor's last patients for the night, so she would be leaving after taking my information, and the doctor would lock up after us. She didn't want us to worry about leaving the doors unlocked behind us when we were done. She said, "The doctor will take care of everything."

I told her how stunned I was that he was working such late hours. Jane informed me that this was a normal, almost daily, occurrence for him. After collecting my information at her desk, she led me back to the waiting room where Emily and Nancy were both sitting quietly. Soon after, Jane left for the night.

In the seats next to us sat a young boy and his mother. The boy appeared to be about eight years old. I figured they were probably still waiting for their appointment, so I thought we must have a while before it was our appointed time with the doctor. I was thankful to be there and would have gratefully and patiently waited all night if needed.

A unique calmness came over me while sitting there in the waiting room. It was most unusual compared to the uneasiness and anxiety that would normally accompany me when waiting in a doctor's office. I started to look around the peaceful waiting area and noticed the beautiful decorations that I had read about in the past. There were religious icons, paintings, and carvings that humbly decorated the office and complemented the holy presence. I now know that each one of these adornments was given to the Nemehs from patients wishing to express their heartfelt gratitude for their healings, fresh beginnings, and/or newly discovered peace. Those sacred treasures were scattered throughout the office to allow others to admire their beauty and become more aware of the faith that fills this place.

As I was noticing the décor, the door opened from the treatment room. An older woman appeared in the doorway. She looked to be in her late sixties and was with a younger man, who I presumed to be her son. When they came out of the room together, the woman slowly stretched out a cane to make her way out of the office. My heart ached once I noticed how far bent over she was as she started walking towards me. Her back was bent over at a forty-five-degree angle. She had lovely, long white hair and her eyes were focused down on the floor as she was shuffling her feet near us. Once she began crossing the floor right in front of me, she turned her head ever so slightly to the right, causing her gaze to shift from the floor to look up at me. She continued staring at me with each shuffle of her feet. Her gaze held onto mine as she slowly passed by with her cane in one hand and her son holding onto the other.

The amount of pain in this woman's eyes was most visible to me. I would guess that anyone watching how she moved would see that she was in a lot of pain. What happened to grab my attention most was there appeared to be a sadness that was communicated simply from looking into her eyes. The look she gave me went straight into my soul. I continued thinking about her as she walked out of sight and left the building. I remember how small I felt at this moment. I closed my eyes and asked myself, *How can I possibly be here wasting this doctor's precious time for something so insignificant as color blindness? I do not deserve to be here.*

Trying to shake these feelings of unworthiness, I slowly reopened my eyes. I noticed the lady and her son had left the door partially open to the treatment room when leaving. I tried to peer inside searching for a glimpse of the doctor. I couldn't seem to find him. A few seconds later, I saw him walking in the back area of the office. Considering I never spotted him coming through the door into the waiting area, I figured he must have escaped the room by another route that was hidden from our sight.

A few minutes later, Dr. Nemeh peeked through the open door. He smiled at all of us sitting there, and then invited the young mom and her son to come join him inside. None of us had spoken a word while sitting in the waiting room together. I know Emily and I were mostly still in awe that we would soon be one-on-one with Dr. Nemeh in the treatment room.

At this point, Nancy began shifting and had trouble sitting. The pain in her back that radiated down her leg became unbearable the longer we sat there. As we waited for our appointment, Emily and I tried to distract Nancy from her pain. We showed her books we found lying on the end tables nearby containing patients' personal miracle stories. The books were full of patient letters, many handwritten, to the Nemehs. The hundreds of letters were presented in a chronicled storybook of sorts. All of the incredible and miraculous testimonies were written in appreciation of the doctor's service to God and others. People clearly poured out their heart and soul in sharing their individual stories, and some of them moved me to tears. Emily and I each had a separate book in hand, and neither one of us was able to put it down. As the minutes went by, we were both totally immersed, going through story after story, frequently calling out, "Wow, you have to read this one!"

These stories seemed to distract Nancy from her pain and lift us up in hope. All three of us continued to pray and read these beautiful miracle stories as we waited until the doctor was ready to see us.

Lamentations 3:25-26 (NRSV)
The Lord is good to those who wait for Him, to the soul that seeks Him. It is good that one should wait quietly for the salvation of the Lord.

three.

Knock, and the Door Will Be Opened

THE MOMENT WE HAD been waiting for had happily arrived. The door to the treatment room opened with Dr. Nemeh holding it open as the mother and son vacated the room. The doctor said goodbye to them as they passed by, turning his focus towards us. He invited the three of us to come into the room with a friendly "hello," a wave of his hand, and a warm smile. As we stood up from our seats, I glanced at the time on my phone, noting it was precisely 11:00 p.m.

Once we passed through the door, I noticed the room was charming, cozy, and simple. To my left was the treatment chair reserved for the patient with a large picture window behind it overlooking the parking lot and the surroundings of the building. On the right side of the chair was an audio-visual (AV) cart. A laptop rested on the top shelf with the shelves below housing various medical tools. To the left of the chair stood a small stereo system near the inside wall, which quietly played instrumental music that gently flowed throughout the room.

On the other side of the room were three empty chairs, all facing in the direction of the designated patient. These strategically placed chairs provided guests with the ability to observe everything that happened with the patient. Behind these chairs, I discovered an additional wall that contained a private door through which the doctor more than likely escaped earlier.

As I studied this space, I noticed some similarities with the waiting room. Religious items and icons, most of which appeared Catholic in nature, hung on walls and sat on shelves. The doctor visibly demonstrated his faith by displaying these items. They serve as a steady reminder for patients and visitors alike to appreciate where Dr. Nemeh's faith truly lies.

I was still trying to comprehend that I was really standing there and recognized I hadn't moved an inch since stepping inside the room. I watched as the doctor approached the sink that was located across the room from the entrance and began to run water and lather his hands. He appeared cheerful, happily smiling and welcoming us, while thoughtfully asking questions regarding our long drive to Ohio. He motioned for Nancy and Emily to sit in the seats that were still empty. At his prompting, I realized it wasn't only me who hadn't moved, but they appeared as captivated as I was by where we were standing.

Dr. Nemeh requested I remove my socks and shoes, as well as roll up my pants. I did as he asked, while noticing that when he was cleaning his hands, he was gazing up towards the ceiling. I followed my eyes to the area where he was studying but was not able to locate or grasp what appeared to have his attention. He grabbed a few paper towels, dried his hands, and asked me to have a seat in the treatment chair. As I walked up to the blue, cushy chair that was sitting straight and tall, I recognized how it had the potential to be adjusted and recline back. I hopped up into the chair and glanced over to Emily and Nancy. They both sat in their seats and smiled up at me while watching Dr. Nemeh's every move with the utmost curiosity.

Dr. Nemeh is a licensed medical doctor with specialties in both anesthesiology and general surgery. I read that he has been practicing medicine in Ohio for over thirty years where he primarily treats and diagnoses patients, working with Meridian Regulatory Acupuncture, which is quite different from Chinese Acupuncture. Meridian Acupuncture has more to do with the electrical resistance of the body. However, most who know Dr. Nemeh understand the healings come straight from God through the doctor's many prayers and steadfast faith.

As Dr. Nemeh began, he gave me an electrical ground to hold in my left hand while he worked on me. He began testing using a small probe, by placing it along various meridian points on my body for short periods of time, normally lasting only one or two seconds. I felt no discomfort whatsoever. This process was repeatedly done over my limbs, hands, feet, face, back, stomach, and neck.

From what I have come to learn about Dr. Nemeh, a depiction of the patient's current health and illnesses are spiritually given to him through the Holy Spirit. I knew all of this prior to going into my appointment from the vast amount of research I had done on him beforehand. Even so, I also understood that he would still be incorporating medical devices during the visit. I, personally, believe he uses medical instruments as a way to help open a patient's mind to understand that a healing is truly possible. These tools allow our thinking to connect to the spiritual level by physically letting our eyes see an object. When truthfully, all Dr. Nemeh needs to use is prayer.

It reminds me of the story in the Bible of Jesus and the blind man. Jesus places mud on the man's eyes before his vision is restored. Did Jesus need the mud for the prayer to work? Absolutely not. The *man* needed the mud as a tool to help facilitate the healing in his body. Feeling the mud helped the man reach the right state of mind to allow his physical consciousness to remove any barriers and connect to the healing itself. This is the same concept I associate with what I have learned from Dr. Nemeh this past year, which is that the healing takes place first in the mind, your physical consciousness, and then manifests itself into the body and soul.

The most helpful information I learned that helped prepare me for my appointment with Dr. Nemeh was discovering that he remains in constant, unspoken prayers for the person who is in front of him. While he is visibly performing the testing, he is also privately praying for his patient. Since this act of kindness and love is virtually undetectable, most often, it is usually not observed by the patient. The majority of patients have no idea he is offering such a tremendous gift to them. This prior knowledge gave me insight and the utmost respect for what was invisibly taking place during my time with him.

One of the most impressive traits that I observed while watching Dr. Nemeh was how he carried himself. It is quite obvious how he loves and cares for each person placed in front of him. He has a way of demonstrating this capacity simply by the way he looks at each person. He is most gentle and quiet in nature. Dr. Nemeh is an incredibly humble man who has dedicated his entire life to God and serving others. He is clearly a servant of our Lord.

Ephesians 4:2 (NRSV)

With all humility and gentleness, with patience, bearing with one another in love.

four.

A Blessed Reason

D R. NEMEH CONTINUED TAKING initial readings that were registered onto a machine, which provided him with data that I couldn't comprehend. As he remained preoccupied, I grew exceedingly fidgety. The concerns I had earlier of being "unfit" to be there were taking over. I felt unworthy, as if I was wasting this doctor's most valuable time. Considering the fact that some who came to see him were suffering with stage IV cancers, serious and deadly diseases, and unrelenting painful conditions was troubling me.

Here I sat, with at the very worst, a disease that was pretty much successfully being treated with medication. I couldn't shake these concerns I was having about how selfish I felt to be there. Each time I would conclude that it was a mistake to be there. These feelings became so overwhelming that I inadvertently blurted out to the doctor that I didn't feel worthy to be there. His reply took me by surprise. He looked up at me with a kind smile and said, "You are *supposed* to be here. You are here for a blessed reason."

This took my breath away. *A blessed reason?* I marveled to myself.

I reasoned that he must have known something that I didn't. *Perhaps something more serious was wrong with me?* I wondered. I wasn't sure what it all meant, but what I did know was that I would never forget those touching words of his. Soon after saying these kind words, he turned around on his chair to look over at my friend Nancy. She was no longer sitting but was now standing and leaning up against the wall. He pointed to the chair indicating that she could sit down and didn't need to stand. She looked nervous and appeared hesitant to mention the pain radiating down her leg. I had no doubt this pain was what led her to stand.

After a few moments of silence, I suddenly interjected, explaining her condition. He laid down the instrument he was using on me, stood up, and walked directly to her. He stood behind her and asked her a few simple questions first. Then he extended his hands over her back and leg and began praying. Emily and I exchanged looks of admiration of what Dr. Nemeh was doing for Nancy. His loving and caring nature allowed her pain to move his heart, drawing him over to her to offer prayers of assistance.

The doctor told Nancy her back was spreading apart, saying it became like putty in his hands. He proclaimed God was healing her. After a few seconds, she informed us that she felt an unusual sensation moving in her back. Nancy appeared apprehensive, like she couldn't completely understand what was taking place. She was both crying and laughing simultaneously. The three of us were moved to tears as Dr. Nemeh continued praying for her.

He asked her to walk around after he was finished. She did so, noting the pain was considerably less, but not completely gone. He asked her to come back over to him, and then he prayed again, asking her to walk around once more. She reported even more improvement. The doctor grinned and returned back over towards me.

Nancy and Emily were both giggling and talking between themselves about the strange sensations Nancy felt. I heard her repeating how weird it was. She felt actual movement inside her back while he was praying. Not realizing it, Nancy walked up to her chair and sat down as she described how it felt to Emily with much enthusiasm in her voice. It was clear to me she felt much better.

Dr. Nemeh was working on taking more readings with the machine, and while doing so, he walked in front of me and noticed something that appeared "off." He made a comment about my left knee being crooked. He commented, "Don't worry. We will fix that later."

I looked over at my daughter with a most puzzled look on my face. I was confused about both of those comments. First, that my knee was crooked, and if so, how had I never noticed such a peculiar issue in my own body before? And second, he claimed he would "*fix*" it later. *What did he mean by that exactly?* I asked myself. With a cute smile, Emily indicated how amused she was by his odd comment and my confused look.

I took a good look at my knee. I was stunned to notice that he was indeed correct. My kneecap was not at all centered! Dr. Nemeh discussed this issue more in-depth by explaining how the position of the knee affects the way a person walks and balances, which, if crooked or off-centered, could lead to pain in the spine and other health complications, similar to some of the problems I had been experiencing.

Emily stood up and took a few steps closer towards me to get a better look at my knee from her perspective. She exclaimed, "Oh wow, it *is* crooked!"

We all laughed that I had never noticed this obvious misalignment in my whole life. It was especially strange since my knee wasn't only slightly crooked, it was *far* off to the right from the center of the joint.

Dr. Nemeh was standing behind me, continuing to acquire more electrical readings on my back. While he was working, all of a sudden, I *felt* my left kneecap move sideways back to the center of my knee all on its own. It happened so quickly as if it were sucked back into place by a vacuum. No one was touching it or even in front of me to position it there. For a split second, I could not understand what had just happened. I examined my knee, and there it was sitting perfectly centered. I started to nervously laugh, similar to Nancy's laugh earlier. I said more to myself than to anyone else, "Oh wow!! My knee just moved! That was so weird!"

And then I heard a small, quiet laugh come from Dr. Nemeh behind me. The room then became silent for a few seconds. Emily broke the silence exclaiming, "Really?!" as she came closer to get another view.

Emily and Nancy began laughing at the unusual incident that had just taken place. No explanation was given by the doctor as to what had happened, and none was needed. I was well aware of the power of Dr. Nemeh's faith and prayers. Miracles happened all around him day and night. However, I was still in shock. It is one thing to read about someone else's miracles that can only be explained by God's intervention, but it is quite another to actually experience them for yourself.

Shortly after this remarkable event, the doctor stood up, turned on his heel, and looked back at Nancy. He was checking in with her to ask how she was feeling. I briefly explained to him that she had recently had a mastectomy and was going through chemotherapy and other treatments.

Dr. Nemeh gave a compassionate glance towards her, expressing his sadness at her recent trials. He began asking her a litany of health questions. She answered all his questions and gave additional details regarding the fact that this was her second round of cancer recurring in the same location.

Then Dr. Nemeh asked Nancy if she had any numbness as a result of the mastectomy. Since the surgery required the removal of lymph nodes, it severed all the nerve endings around the surrounding area. As a consequence, Nancy was in fact experiencing numbness, just as Dr. Nemeh suspected. This life-saving surgery caused Nancy to lose all sensation along her side. Nancy's surgeon made it clear that she would never regain feeling in this area because, "Nerves don't grow back."

We could tell by the expression on the doctor's face that he was inspired to pray even more for her healing. Dr. Nemeh extended his right hand, pointed his fingers towards the nerve damage, and bowed his head in prayer. Nancy looked up, not realizing where the doctor had placed his hand, and began to cry. Then Nancy excitedly exclaimed, "I can feel something touching me! Something is rubbing me there!"

Little did Nancy know the doctor's hand was in midair, hovering inches away from her. She continued saying it over and over. Emily and I both happily called out in unison, "He's not touching you."

Dr. Nemeh was now beaming and said softly, "Perhaps you feel Jesus rubbing you, because I'm not touching you."

The three of us gave out a joy-filled cry! What was unfolding in front of our eyes was indeed a true miracle! There was no pathway for Nancy's nerves to transmit or to perceive such a sensation. This confirmed that her sense of touch had been marvelously restored, and it has remained ever since.

During this most heartwarming experience, I remained seated in my chair and was in the process of wiping away my tears when I noticed the doctor move towards me to continue the treatment. He sat behind me, out of my view, and began directing prayers towards my left shoulder. I heard him begin with faint whispers, "Come Holy Spirit...in the name of Jesus..."

My left shoulder was a great source of pain for me. Not only did I have lupus, but I also had many other autoimmune issues that had surfaced in recent years, one of which was fibromyalgia. I had been diagnosed with it several years prior. It caused many painful, tender knots throughout my left shoulder, back, and neck. It progressively worsened throughout the years, leading me to ask my husband and children on a daily basis to gently help rub out the knots. This pain had become my "new normal."

Dr. Nemeh didn't need me to say a word concerning the pain or about having fibromyalgia; he just knew. After he had finished praying, he stood back and asked me how my shoulder felt. Trying to evaluate it, I began wiggling it up and down and winding my arm like I was preparing to pitch a ball. Thrilled, I reported to him all the pain was completely gone! To this day, I have never had any pain or a single knot return. Thanks be to God!

At times when the doctor was praying, I felt like we were also in the presence of Jesus, as if He were standing right beside the doctor as he moved all throughout the room. Often I wondered if Jesus was really present in a way that only Dr. Nemeh could see, since I would catch the doctor staring to some far-off location behind me, like he was looking past our physical world. It was as if God had focused his attention towards Heaven. As I watched him fix his gaze to a distant place one more time, I couldn't help but marvel at the idea that he was looking upon something or someone that was invisible to the rest of us in the room. He interrupted my curious thinking by asking me how I was feeling. He directly asked about symptoms that correlated with fibromyalgia and Raynaud's Syndrome, without necessarily naming the conditions.

Dr. Nemeh had completed his diagnostic testing on me and was setting up the next phase, the Meridian Acupuncture itself. He described what to expect with the process, along with suggesting that from here on out I would feel much warmer in my hands and feet. Trying to clarify, I asked if he was referring to the symptoms specifically related to me having Raynaud's Syndrome. His reply was, "Yes. They will be completely healed."

His words left me speechless. Then Dr. Nemeh started to discuss the healing of my knee and its restored location. He suggested investing in new shoes as soon as possible. Since my shoes were adjusted to my original balance, they now might cause me to step incorrectly, possibly injuring myself. He warned me to be cautious since my walking and stability would be different.

As he was addressing my newfound step, he stopped in mid-sentence and took notice of the index finger on my left hand. He asked me what I had done to it. I told him I had a simple but painful papercut. I probably gave him more details than he needed, or probably ever wanted.

In the midst of my babbling, he held his hand slightly above my finger and began to pray. I stopped speaking and waited to see what would happen next. As I was trying not to blink so that I could observe his every move and keep an eye on my finger, I watched a scab form right in front of my eyes immediately covering my sore, healing it within a matter of seconds. I could not believe my eyes!

Dr. Nemeh didn't dwell on how the scab seemingly appeared out of thin air, he simply moved on to other matters, and was now inquiring if I had any bladder issues. Being in total shock to his awareness and the question, I paused and then responded, "Yes. Yes, as a matter of fact I do."

I was stunned because I had only shared this issue with one other person, and that was Emily. I had never told my husband or any of my doctors. The doctor continued probing, "Do you have cramping with your bladder? Does it keep you awake at night?"

I answered, "Yes and yes," while still admiring his unique yet profound perception.

He informed me that this too would be "fixed," and he added that if he didn't address the problem, it would develop into something worse. "Eventually this problem you are having would have progressed into interstitial cystitis, for which there is no cure," he concluded.

He went on to tell me that I would be able to sleep straight through the night from here on out. After hearing this startling information, I found myself all the more thankful for his amazing insights, as well as relieved that he had addressed this situation, especially since I never planned on mentioning it.

I decided this would be a good time to mention my symptoms of color blindness. He listened attentively to the details of my autoimmune situation, which is what ultimately led me to schedule an appointment with him. Without speaking, he walked across the room and picked up a rather shiny and smooth object that reminded me of a small metal boomerang. He asked me to keep my eyes closed and rubbed it gently over each one. This unique tool he used contained prickly points on its surface, which felt like a gentle brushstroke against each eyelid. The sensation startled me at first, but never triggered any pain. He finished, and at his request, I looked around the room, and I was able to differentiate numerous colors like never before. I was able to accurately identify all shades and colors perfectly! I am still able to detect a full range of colors to this day. Praise God!

Dr. Nemeh proceeded to ask how many children I had. I was not prepared for *this* question. I didn't know how to answer him or what to say. I looked up away from him and shot a look over to Emily and smiled because I have a painful past that concerns this particular subject. The wounds have been tucked away, and in truth, I've never thoroughly dealt with them very well. As Emily and I traded looks, Dr. Nemeh apparently noticed this peculiar, silent exchange and asked me with a kind-hearted smile, "What?"

I had this feeling that one way or another, he already understood my hesitation. I felt no judgment from him whatsoever, but I felt like he knew all about my past and could sense the deep pain and loss I have carried in my heart every day. I took a moment before speaking, smiled back at him, and ambiguously said, "Oh nothing. It's complicated."

Still smiling and in a very sweet and loving voice, he replied, "Mysteries."

At this point, he was finished with my treatment for the night. As Dr. Nemeh advanced his way over to Nancy to pray one last time for her, Emily and I both stood up to see what would happen next. He asked if there were any more sensations occurring with this latest set of prayers regarding her back and leg pain. She described a warm, tingling phenomenon developing down her leg. She kept repeating how strange it felt.

All at once, he changed the subject by asking, "Did you know that your hips were tilted?"

Nancy was caught off guard by the question. She began to laugh nervously a little, while admitting that she had recently discovered this fact. Without any hesitation, he went into deep prayer, and as we watched, her right hip physically swung forward and upward in one swift and gentle motion all on its own. Dr. Nemeh matter-of-factly said, "There you go."

The three of us were astounded at the various miracles we had witnessed that evening. The doctor passed by Nancy and headed over to my daughter. He asked Emily her age and what she did, all the while slowly and quietly sliding a chair up behind her as he spoke with her. She replied, "Nineteen, and I am a sophomore at the University of Northern Iowa studying Elementary Education."

I noticed Emily had tears starting to well in her eyes as if she already understood that Dr. Nemeh was about to pray over her as well. She was humbled and overwhelmed by his generosity to pray for her. He began, "Come Holy Spirit, through Your Beloved Son...Come Lord Jesus."

Emily immediately had the Holy Spirit come upon her, and she rested back into the chair ever so gently. Her eyes were closed, and she began breathing deeply. Her head leaned back some, while Dr. Nemeh's hands drifted over her spine, neck, and lower back. She looked incredibly peaceful sitting back in the chair as the doctor was continually murmuring prayers for a while longer. Emily's back became straighter and taller in the chair; it appeared as if she grew several inches right in front of my eyes. It was a lovely and powerful encounter to watch. Dr. Nemeh proceeded to direct his prayers over Emily's abdomen. He prayed for a while, appearing to know precisely where her issues were located.

Many tears fell from my eyes while I gazed on this beautiful scene playing out in front of me. I was doing my best to unite my prayers with the doctor's, praying for Emily to be perfectly healed. Once he was finished, Emily's eyes began to open. I noticed she was moved by this profound encounter, because she never stopped shedding tears from the moment Dr. Nemeh had started praying over her. With that, the doctor gave one of his telling smiles, looked at the three of us, and softly pronounced he was finished for the night, and it was therefore time for us to leave. He reminded us of my appointment with him the following morning at 11:00 a.m. We gathered our belongings, continually dabbing away at our tears.

The entire visit was filled with many unique experiences that I had never felt, seen, or even imagined were possible. Everything that night was unfamiliar to me, even time itself. I had no idea how long it had been since we stepped foot in that special office. I glanced at my phone as I put on my coat and saw that it was now 1:15 a.m. I was stunned! We had been inside the treatment room for over two solid hours. Each moment we had spent with Dr. Nemeh touched my soul and showed me that *anything* is truly possible with God.

In awe, all three of us headed out the door to go outside. The cold air and the light flurries hinted that the blizzard from the west was close at hand. The doctor's wife, Kathy, pulled into the parking spot next to our car. She came to pick up her husband and take him home for the night. When she rolled down her window and I was able to recognize her, it felt like I was reuniting with a close friend, even though I didn't truly know her. There is something quite extraordinary about Kathy that has made such an impression on me each time.

She called out to us, asking how the time went with the doctor. We each exclaimed similar words, "Amazing!" "Beautiful!" "Wonderful!" all while *trying* our best to describe an evening unlike any other.

Kathy nodded, and with a cheerful smile acclaimed, "It's amazing, isn't it?"

She asked what hotel we were staying in for the night. I informed her where and that we were barely ten minutes away. My answer appeared to give her an instant sense of relief that we didn't have so far to drive. I could tell she worried about the upcoming snow resulting in unsafe, messy roads. She asked if it would be okay to move my appointment back to 12:00 p.m. the next day, since the weather updates were predicting the snowstorm would come rapidly, possibly overnight. She thought this would give the street crews a chance to clean up the roads. Her sense of caring for others ran as deep as her husband's.

Deuteronomy 10:21 (NRSV)
He is your praise; He is your God, who has done for you these great and awesome things that your own eyes have seen.

five.

What Did You See?

WE WOKE UP SATURDAY morning, surprised that the blizzard that was expected to come overnight had been delayed. At first, I thought maybe it had missed us, but I later discovered that the meteorologists had changed their forecast, rescheduling the storm's arrival still for Saturday, but later in the afternoon and evening. I worried this delay would make traveling more difficult for our trip home tomorrow after the healing service with Dr. Nemeh. The service was being held at a hotel just down the road from where we were presently staying. I tried to stay hopeful that by attending the service early Sunday morning, it would give the storm a little extra time to blow over before we were to begin driving back home to Iowa.

Fortunately, the delay allowed us to have a nice, safe drive over to the doctor's office on Saturday morning, even though nearly an inch of snow had already accumulated on the ground. It was a typical, cold January day with the temperatures hovering in the low twenties. We were all bundled up in our standard winter gear to stay warm. However, I was experiencing intermittent chills, on and off, from the overall anticipation of this second appointment, especially considering what had happened yesterday.

We arrived at the doctor's office just before noon, before anyone else had arrived, including the staff and the doctor himself. Nancy, Emily, and I sat in the car sipping away on some strong, hot coffee that we had picked up at a Starbucks along the way. We were all eagerly awaiting this second appointment, knowing full well the possibilities were endless.

Kathy Nemeh pulled into the parking lot with the doctor in the passenger seat. They arrived shortly after we did. When they opened their car doors, I noticed both of them were also drinking from the signature white and green paper cups from Starbucks. We all hopped out of our vehicles, and the five of us walked into the office together. Kathy chatted with us along the way inside, asking how each of us was feeling. Of course, there were no words to express the immensity of love, joy, and peace we each held in our hearts other than by saying, "Absolutely incredible!"

The doctor simply smiled and cheerfully said, "Good Morning."

The three of us filed back into the treatment room, the place where we had experienced Heaven on earth the night before. As we were settling in, we took great care to place our coffee cups, purses, coats, hats, and gloves out of the doctor's path. In addition, I removed my snow-covered shoes and socks as he once more requested of me.

It appeared the doctor was ready to get straight to work. He was standing in front of the sink washing up when he kindly asked how I had slept and how I was feeling. I reported with much joy in my heart, "Extremely well... on both accounts."

I was in awe that for the first time in years, I could honestly say that I felt *well*. As I was still thinking about my current health, Nancy asked Dr. Nemeh how he had slept, to which he replied, "Good."

Nancy suggested that he must sleep well most nights since he works long hours and doesn't have much time for sleep. He looked up from the sink, with a troubled look on his face and answered, "No, I do not."

There was a slight pause, and then he went on to say, "I have a lot of things that I am thinking about always. I have lots to do. I am very busy. I need only two to maybe four hours of sleep each night. God made me special that way."

He responded with such great sincerity in his voice, which made me think there must be many things weighing on his heart and mind, and in all likelihood, within his soul as well. Following this exchange, he was ready to begin his work and invited me to sit in the patient chair. He was smiling, but then he became more serious and contemplative rather quickly, as if he was still thinking about whatever he was alluding to when he answered Nancy's question.

He began this appointment much the same way as the night before, using the same probing instruments. Lightheartedly, he then asked about my paper cut. I told him how I was still amazed at how it had scabbed right over in front of my eyes the night before. Then I lifted my finger to show him what I had done to it in the shower afterwards. I had bumped it and the scab fell off causing it to bleed all over again. Dr. Nemeh declared while laughing, "It will be fixed. Don't worry."

Turning himself around, he checked in with Nancy by asking how her back and leg were doing. She reluctantly admitted that despite the prayers, she was still a bit sore. He stood up and attended to her. Now weeping, Nancy cried, "I am so sorry that it didn't heal."

Dr. Nemeh contended, "You *were* healed. This is only an irritated muscle, and it will take a while for it to completely heal and feel better."

After he had finished praying and talking with her, he returned towards me, displaying his usual, pleasant smile. He retrieved a wand-like instrument, brought it over, and held it above my finger for a minute. It somewhat resembled a flashlight, but it did not give off any detectable light, nor did I pick up on any sensation associated with it. As I waited to find out what would happen next, I foolishly asked him, "Is this instrument healing my finger?"

He chuckled at my absurd question, claiming it was a combination between science and prayer. He reinforced what he meant by clarifying, "With prayer, I could use a twig from a tree and your finger would be healed!"

This prompted Dr. Nemeh to discuss many other miraculous stories, mostly involving the healing of skeptics and the background behind their healings. He described that by the end of their appointments, these same people were moved to tears by the miracles manifesting in front of their very own eyes. I had no doubt about any of these accounts, especially after everything we had witnessed.

One of the most memorable stories he shared with us was about a child who was born without any retinas. Her vision was fully restored after receiving a prayer from Dr. Nemeh. She still retains her vision to this day, even without having retinas. By all means, this young girl shouldn't be able to see anything, physically speaking, but it doesn't make any difference. There are no limits with God.

Dr. Nemeh then transitioned to a discussion about the relationship between God and science. He spoke about the quantum field and how so many people are confused by it. "The quantum field is essentially God's mind," he said. "We can connect with it, with God, if we let go of our own will and surrender to God's will."

Dr. Nemeh provided us with an entirely different perspective about spiritual matters. He explained that how he sees it, evil is becoming weaker, not stronger, as most people claim. Specifically, he proposed that when a believer or someone with true love in their heart surrenders their life to Christ, they begin to block out evil influences and the fallen angels, one at a time.

Once the number of believers, which is the body of Christ, matches the number of fallen angels, evil on this earth will be done. Evil knows its time is short and thus at times falsely appears as if evil is growing in intensity, however, the reality is it is only becoming more public because it is desperate. He also referred to "the end of times" saying, "Jesus is coming soon. All the signs and visions that are happening all over the world point to it, but only the Father knows the exact day and time."

He provided so many incredible pieces of information that I could barely keep up. Much of the wisdom he offered answered questions that

Emily and I had wondered about for years. Dr. Nemeh was full of wisdom and truth. It was like a breath of fresh air for our souls.

Afterwards, he became increasingly quiet. At this time, I was still sitting upright in the chair as he stepped back to the right behind me. Upon trying to glance back at him, I happened to take notice that the back of the chair had been extended down, transforming it into more of a reclining table than a chair.

Dr. Nemeh was largely hidden from my view; as a result, I wasn't able to see anything he was doing, nor could I hear any noise coming from him. Slowly, I felt my eyes gently closing all on their own. Simultaneously, I also detected an irresistible tug from within me to lie back. Struggling to stay upright, I managed to reopen my eyes while doing my best to shake off this unexpected sensation. I was afraid that if I were to lie back, I would fall over onto the doctor since I wasn't sure if he was paying close attention to me or what he was doing behind me.

I continually fought the urge to recline back as it beckoned me over and over again. I attempted to peer at the doctor behind me another time, but I still couldn't make out what he was doing. This time, however, as I brought my gaze forward over to Emily, I realized that *she* could see him and seemed very excited about what she was observing.

Suddenly, I was aware that my eyes had, once again, fallen shut. This time, when I felt the same invisible but irresistible pulling sensation to lie back, I started to submit to the urge. I was letting my guard down and worrying less about what would happen if I did. Little by little, I gave in more, allowing myself to slowly tilt back further and further, until my back was slanted and nearly parallel to the table. Nevertheless, I hadn't gone all the way down. I remained hovering a few inches from the table and not entirely level.

With my eyes remaining closed, I began to distinguish something or someone appearing before me. It was a light that had started slowly streaming into the center of my vision. It contained the loveliest white light I had ever seen. Immediately, it began to move closer towards me, becoming clearer and brighter with each movement, shining like a large glowing flame, and blazing against the darkness. Observing this light, I knew that it was sacred in nature. It is very difficult to describe, but spiritually speaking, I knew this light was offering gifts of love and forgiveness, but in order to receive them, I had to be willing to accept them *and surrender everything*.

These gifts were magnificent, but my intellect kept getting in the way. With each offer, I immediately would deem myself unworthy to receive such gifts. Eventually, my physical consciousness took hold, bringing me back to being fully present with my eyes open. I glanced around, now mindful that I remained inches away from lying all the way down, which made me realize how odd this must have been for Nancy and Emily to observe.

Then, ever so gently, my mind was tenderly called back to the same pure and radiant light, prompting my eyes to shut firmly and my mind to be completely fixed on the Holy Glow before me.

The radiant light continually progressed in my direction and began changing into a breathtaking silhouette. The figure was nearly within reach as it manifested from being an outlined profile into a most-divine, three-dimensional person. The person was filled with an even greater light than the illumination that was surrounding Him. As He continued to become more defined, I saw the person of light develop into Christ Himself.

In the exact moment I comprehended and saw who stood before me, my heart inclined toward Him with so much intensity that everything else fell away. My initial resistance to surrender was immediately and completely taken away, allowing me to fall back through the remaining inches of space, to rest upon the chair. All my sensibilities and reasonings that had previously occupied my mind entirely melted away in a single instant. I remained completely mesmerized, and all my attention was on Him who stood before me, the *Prince of Peace*.

Despite the fact that He had a beaming, bright light continually emitting from within Himself, I was able to look directly upon Him. He was clothed in an all-white, ankle-length garment that illuminated white light as well. He stood there staring at me with the most incredible, deep love while also transmitting a sense of peace. Love embodied His very being; it even radiated from His eyes.

Once I realized it was Jesus calling me to receive these offerings of love and mercy, I no longer had any thoughts or worries of being undeserving. He knew everything about me, more than I knew or understood about myself. He was the creator of my soul. I understood that even though He knew *all* things about me, His love still embraced my entire being. I had become utterly and hopelessly swept away by His love. This most merciful act of His also made me very aware of my own soul, where I could essentially *feel* it.

As abundantly as Jesus presented and provided his unconditional, endless love, He also revealed to me that my past transgressions, particularly those where I had not forgiven myself, were gone and forgiven. I could *feel* them leave; it was a most undeserving reconciliation that washed completely over and through me. There were no words being voiced. It was spiritually communicated, leaving me with a peace that was not something of this world. It was unlike any feeling I had ever known.

As I was spiritually observing Jesus and feeling such tremendous love, all of a sudden I was able to audibly hear Dr. Nemeh. He was praying in soft whispers, sitting beside me on my right. I noticed the tears that had been streaming from my eyes for some time were now rolling off my cheeks and onto the table.

I do not know how long this event lasted. Ten minutes? An hour? I believe my sense of time would not be accurate even if I attempted to guess. Time simply tends to stand still and is not easily grasped when Dr. Nemeh is praying, and this is especially true when Jesus is evidently present. During this divine intervention, I wholeheartedly believe I was mysteriously experiencing a small piece of Heaven in that room.

When the moment ended, I slowly opened my eyes that were flooded with tears and turned my head to the right where Dr. Nemeh was barely a breath away, with his head still bowed in prayer for me. As I surveyed the doctor, his eyes began to open, and I noticed they held the same compassionate look to them as Jesus' did. Dr. Nemeh's eyes in some supernatural way carried that same identical love. After spotting this similarity, I started crying even more. I was now sobbing. It was the greatest and holiest experience of my life. Not only did this incredible moment introduce me to a greater awareness of my soul and mark it in a most significant way, but it has also forever changed who I am and how I live my life.

Then, Dr Nemeh said the most thoughtful words that I will always remember, "You have a beautiful soul."

This made me weep. At this point, he was trying to console me. His sympathy for me was obvious. The deep-seated pain I had held onto for most of my life had, in a moment's time, gone and was being carried away by tears. The doctor whispered the word, "Yes," as he acknowledged my emotional state, patting and rubbing my arm in hopes of calming me down.

Quietly, he then asked, "What did you see?"

"Right now?" I asked, still in shock.

He laughed at yet another silly question of mine, responding, "Yes, right now. What did you see?"

I also laughed at my own funny question. Then I described how I had seen Jesus, pouring out his love for me. Dr. Nemeh replied, "Yes. Yes, you did."

He went on to say, "God *knows* about *all* of your children."

I now understood that yesterday, when Emily and I exchanged looks with one another regarding his question about how many children I had, that he already knew the answer. I suspected he knew about all of my children when he asked, but I left well enough alone.

Every single day of my adulthood, my heart had carried around such deep pain and loss concerning adoption procedures that had taken place when I was younger. It had all been tucked away, and in truth, I had never dealt with it very well. It is something I had hardly shared with anyone because it was too heartbreaking for me, until my moment with Dr. Nemeh when Jesus came and so graciously removed all of my grief.

Then he told me the most beautiful thing a mother could ever hope to hear, that my children are saved through prayers.

Dr. Nemeh stated, "God hears us and honors our prayers."

His beautiful words made me cry once again.

Dr. Nemeh went on to say, "You have a beautiful, deep faith. Look how you believed. You drove all the way here. Jesus sees your faith. Keep working and telling others about Jesus. It is important!"

With all of the miraculous healings and heartfelt moments, I wished I never had to leave his office. It felt as if part of my heart was left there and would remain there forever.

When I hopped off the table, my legs were noticeably shaking. All the emotion I felt flooded my body like electricity going straight through me. There was no hiding it. Every aspect of my being was entirely overwhelmed. It was without a doubt, the most incredible and moving encounter of my entire life.

I knew it was almost time for us to leave as he was preparing to say goodbye with his invitation for us to stay in touch regarding the progress of our healings.

I turned to thank Dr. Nemeh for all he had done, and he immediately replied, "Don't thank me. Thank God."

I didn't know what to say because I was genuinely so thankful for being led to this man who had given so much of his time, heart, and prayers to all of us. The generous blessings God bestowed on us in a period of two days made me grateful beyond any measure. I didn't want it to end, but I knew we had to leave.

Deep within myself, I understood I would need some time to sort out what all had taken place. There was so much to think about. I already knew that the most meaningful miracles I had received were not physical in nature. Instead, the most impactful were the emotional healings and spiritual awakenings. God woke me up from sleepwalking through life and enlightened my mind about the unshakable truth and power of living in union with Christ.

Isaiah 38:16-17 (NRSV)
Oh, restore me to health and make me live!
Surely it was for my welfare
that I had great bitterness;
but You have held back my life
from the pit of destruction,
for You have cast all my sins
behind Your back.

six.

I Love You, Jesus

DURING THE LAST FEW minutes before we walked out of Dr. Nemeh's office, he made a statement that at the time appeared random. Dr. Nemeh spoke to no one in particular claiming, "Jesus *knows* you love Him. You don't need to tell Him over and over."

When he made this announcement it seemed to come out of nowhere since none of us were talking whatsoever.

On our way over to the hotel, Nancy gave us a better understanding as to why the doctor would say something that, at the time, seemed odd and out of sorts. Nancy mentioned that after Jesus appeared to me and she witnessed my emotional state, she began repeatedly saying over and over in her head, "I love you, Jesus. I love you, Jesus. I love you, Jesus."

We acknowledged that Dr. Nemeh, in all probability, had heard her thoughts. This was his clever way of reminding us that we do not need to use words. Our feelings of love for each other and for Jesus say it all.

It was such a valuable lesson for us, while at the same time, it made us appreciate yet another form of Dr. Nemeh's connection with Christ.

This event helped us to stay centered on more lighthearted topics, since we weren't quite ready to talk about the more meaningful and profound events that had happened. It was as if our souls needed a breather to process what had taken place, and our brains were, at this point, placed on pause because of it. We chose to honor our high-spirited moment by eating brunch at the Cheesecake Factory, especially since it was conveniently located right across the street from our hotel.

Although the temperature outside was still freezing cold, my hands were incredibly warm just as Dr. Nemeh said they would be. For the first time in years, instead of wearing my gloves, I carried them instead. In the past, I had never dared to do this, even in slightly cool temperatures, because my low circulation would trigger an attack on my hands from a decrease in blood flow, resulting in throbbing pain and loss of skin color.

Emily noticed my new, playful way of sporting my gloves, clutching them in the palms of my hands. She scolded me to wear them the correct way. I knew she worried because the condition I endured before visiting Dr. Nemeh, Raynaud's Syndrome, could potentially damage my blood vessels if I didn't take the necessary precautions. Be that as it may, I was too thrilled at the idea of how warm they felt. I simply believed that I didn't need to wear them.

As we walked into the restaurant, my hands weren't the only thing feeling heated, because each one of our hearts was nearly burning from the joy we felt from everything we had experienced the past couple of days. There were numerous spirit-filled moments that would forever change us if we allowed them to do so. I felt as if I were floating on a cloud from Heaven while striding through the restaurant, following the hostess to our table. Life seemed so perfect in that moment.

Shortly after we placed our order, however, I began to feel sick. A sudden and unexpected wave of nausea hit me. It was bad and only got worse by the minute. I was heartbroken. I had to break the news, and since we were in a restaurant, I tried to be discreet. Leaning over to Emily, who was sitting next to me in the booth, I whispered in her ear that I felt sick and that we should leave, insisting that we needed to do so right away before things took a turn for the worse. She broke the news quietly to Nancy while I struggled to keep myself from crying. I was so sad, having felt wonderful just moments ago, and then in an instant, it was suddenly all stripped away.

We left there with our food in boxes, in a hurry to return to the hotel room. Neither Emily nor Nancy complained about not being able to eat. They were both sympathetic to my situation, kindly not bringing it up.

When we reached our hotel room, we agreed to rest awhile, mostly because we were tired from not having slept the night before on account of our enthusiasm. I lay down on the bed that I shared with Emily and rapidly began to feel better. Looking back over all I have learned since that time, I now know this sick feeling was brought about by the healing that was taking place inside my body.

Nancy began playing a game on her iPad and quickly drifted off to sleep within a few minutes. Emily and I were still alert but quietly at rest. We opted to document every detail, observation, insight, and emotion we had experienced from our time with Dr. Nemeh. We didn't want to lose a single moment. We each had our own personal journals that we had brought from home for this precise reason, and we began putting all these reflections into writing. We wrote for over an hour straight, doing our best to recapture every moment.

Afterwards, as Nancy continued sleeping, we sat next to each other on the bed, quietly whispering to each other, describing what we had felt during our own personal encounters. Emily spoke to me in tears about the sense of incredible peace and love she had felt when being prayed over, and I communicated some of what had happened to me when seeing Jesus. It didn't take long before we decided to get some sleep ourselves, since reviewing these past two days had made our minds even more worn out. There was much to reflect upon, and most of it was so full of meaning that it would take extensive time to do so. I didn't want to overanalyze, but I already knew this was a new beginning for me somehow. I just wasn't sure what it would lead to necessarily.

As I lay there quietly resting, I kept striving to look at the bigger picture. I didn't even know where to begin. I kept replaying the moment with Jesus over in my head. It was unforgettable, forever infused into my mind. I found that most of what had happened to me was hard to place into words or describe when talking to Emily, as there really wasn't an accurate way to convey everything. However, what seemed to speak louder than words was the emotion I felt in my heart, which Emily understood when I spoke to her about the event. I closed my eyes, recapturing it again in my mind as I reflected on that last statement of Dr. Nemeh's, referring to love not needing words. These most loving thoughts shepherded me into sleep over the next several hours.

Upon awakening around supper time, the three of us determined we should go downstairs into the lobby for some fresh air and to stretch our legs a bit before searching for something else to eat. None of us spoke nearly as much as we had the night before. Every so often, however, one of us would make a random comment regarding one of our recent miraculous experiences. These unplanned bursts of dialogue illustrated how our thoughts were still racing, trying to process everything that had taken place.

After stepping off the elevator and entering the lobby, we turned the corner to spot the young woman and her son who had originally been in the waiting room at Dr. Nemeh's office that first night. She was there with one more son who was older, as well as a man, who was undoubtedly her husband and the boys' father. They were seated at one of the tables and had just finished eating their supper only moments earlier.

We went over to introduce ourselves. They were a nice and friendly family. We exchanged stories about how each of us had come to know this special doctor. They never fully disclosed their medical story, but the mother revealed it was purely coincidental how she had come across the book, *Miracles Every Day,* and that she still wondered, "Could all of this be for real?"

The three of us were nodding our heads in answer to what I sensed was a rhetorical question. I then chimed in anyway, rhetorical or not, and with all seriousness to my voice, "Yes! This is all *very much* real."

During our short discussion, most of us were moved to tears. It is hard not to be emotional when talking about personal healings because they touch your very soul.

The mother of the family asked if we were planning to attend the healing service the next morning. I confirmed, that yes, we were indeed going, and then from there we would be on our way home to Iowa. The father of the family informed us that they were, likewise, attending the service, and they had quite a lengthy drive to reach their home as well.

It wasn't long before our conversation went from sentiments of bliss to thoughts of worry about the upcoming day. These troublesome feelings we had were not at all related to the healing service, but they had everything to do with the dicey weather. The long commute we each had to make after the service, with the added potential of having hazardous road conditions, was intimidating. We began talking more about the snowstorm and how odd it was that it kept stalling, since it had once again suspended itself this afternoon, and now was forecast to hit in the overnight hours. The expected "blizzard" that they were calling for had thankfully lessened and was not supposed to be as severe as originally predicted. However, from what they were forecasting, the weather tomorrow would still pose a major threat, which would make it challenging for all of us to get home safely.

Following our brief conversation with this loving family, they decided to go up to their room to rest. Before leaving, they thoughtfully offered us the remains of their takeout food they had purchased from a nearby restaurant. They had a considerable amount left over and decided they were too full to finish what they had left. Given that the weather was starting to become touch-and-go, we thought it would be wise to accept their generous offer instead of venturing back outdoors for another meal. We appreciated running into this sweet family when we did and the instant friendship we seemed to forge with them, especially considering moments before, we had been all but strangers to one another.

The exhaustion from everything started to set back in with me once again. All of it was weighing on every part of me – my mind, heart, and spirit. The emotional and spiritual stirrings were causing my physical body to beg for some more rest. I recommended to Nancy and Emily that we should go up to our room and try to relax. They both appeared grateful for my suggestion, and we made a beeline straight to our room.

While lying in bed that night, I remembered that prior to coming on this trip, Emily and I had both compiled a list of all the health issues we had been suffering from. Curiously, I wondered how many of my health problems would be healed. This list presented a way for us to keep track of any changes. It sounds funny, but so often when a person has pain or is not feeling well, they take notice of it right away because the pain calls attention to it. On the contrary, when an ailment leaves their body, a person can mysteriously fail to remember, and after a while, may even forget all about ever having had it in the first place. We wanted to be sure we wouldn't forget.

The following is a list of my health concerns before going to Ohio:

- Systemic lupus
- Fevers of unknown origin
- Knots and pain in left shoulder, back, and neck
- Arthritic pain and swelling in hands and wrists

- Jaw pain and clenching (TMJ)
- Migraines
- Dizziness
- Extreme itchiness over head and torso
- Unexplainable rashes
- Concentration and memory problems ("lupus fog")
- Painful bladder contractions
- Color blindness
- Fibromyalgia
- Mouth ulcers
- Raynaud's Syndrome
- Weakness in legs at night – difficulty climbing stairs
- Daily muscle cramps in feet
- Lack of peace/anxiety
- Gluten intolerance
- Small intestinal bacterial overgrowth (S.I.B.O.)
- Lack of forgiveness of self
- Deep emotional trauma from childhood

Over time, I would discover that each one of these health/emotional concerns was either completely healed or minimized, even to this day. Just as God calls us to love Him deeply within the silence of our hearts, I believe He chooses to heal and sustain us in the same way. In the silence of our hearts.

1 John 3:18 (NRSV)

Let us love, not in word or speech, but in truth and action.

seven.

Sharing the Good News

WE WOKE UP EARLY Sunday morning, excited about attending the healing service. Wondering if the snowstorm had come overnight, I glanced out the window of the hotel to have a look. *It had most definitely arrived*, I thought as I caught sight of the white snow blanketing the streets. As lovely as the outside landscape now appeared, decorated in the beautiful fresh snow, I knew the reality of our drive back home would not be so pretty.

We were hoping to leave a little early from the service to make it home by a decent hour that night, so Nancy and I would be rested enough to return to work on Monday and Emily would be able to attend her classes. On good roads, it was close to a nine-hour drive, but with the uncertainty of the travel conditions, I was concerned how the new snow and strong winds might prolong our ride home.

The three of us cleaned up, packed our bags, and checked out of the hotel as fast as we could. We wanted to leave some extra time to pick up our morning coffee and breakfast along the way over to the service. It was freezing cold out, and none of us were in the talking mood just yet. It wasn't that we didn't have anything to talk about necessarily, but I think we were still overwhelmed and needed more time to process. After eating breakfast at a local coffeehouse, we drove a few miles to the hotel where the service was being held.

When pulling into the hotel's snow-covered parking lot, I wondered how many people would be able to make it, since the snowstorm had finally arrived through the overnight hours. Thankfully, it moved in, and then disappeared just about as fast as it came, leaving only a trace of flurries drifting from the sky.

As we hurried into the hotel to get out of the cold, we made our way directly to the conference room where the service was to be held. I noticed there had been a few changes since I had last attended a Dr. Nemeh healing service. The room was still set up in the familiar theater-style seating; however, chairs had now been added to the front of the room for those receiving a prayer. They no longer laid people down if they fell in the Spirit. The volunteers now would guide them safely to rest in a chair.

The healing service started out with Kathy introducing her husband and asking that we each come up with faith, hope, and courage when going up for our individual prayers. Then, Dr. Nemeh gave a brief inspirational talk about faith, explaining the largest mystery for us is that God is a Trinity – the Father, the Son, and the Holy Spirit. This Trinity equals a unity. He related that as we have a brain, a body, and a soul – we are a part of that unity. We experience God the Father through the manifestations of the Holy Spirit, and Jesus is the absolute center of each one.

Kathy Nemeh knew we had a long drive back home to Iowa, and so thoughtfully asked us to come up for our prayers right away. She recognized with the uncertainty of the roads that we needed to begin our travels as soon as possible. As Dr. Nemeh approached Emily and me, he gave us a warm smile and offered a hug to say, *"hello"* again. When praying over us, we each momentarily fell in the Spirit. I noticed Nancy had a familiar expression on her face; it was the same look I had seen on Randy back in 2011. Nancy appeared to be struggling with surrendering to God, just as Randy had eight years earlier. Nancy, however, was emotional and shedding countless tears. At one point, I saw Dr. Nemeh's eyes fill with tears as well. I wasn't sure if this was because he felt her pain or was saddened by how Nancy just couldn't seem to let go. Perhaps it was a little bit of both. After he finished praying over Nancy, Emily and I found a seat to watch the service for a few more minutes before leaving for home. We found two seats next to each other in the very front row.

We decided to stay a little longer because we recognized someone that was in line to receive a prayer soon. This person was the very same bent-over woman we had seen coming out of Dr. Nemeh's office when we had first arrived on Friday evening. Today she was sitting next to her son with cane in hand, waiting for her prayer. As we sat there in the front row, we eagerly waited to see what would happen when Dr. Nemeh prayed for her. Emily and I continually prayed for her healing and for her to feel God's love.

As Dr. Nemeh approached her, he asked her to please stand up. We heard him say in the most tender and caring way, "You have been suffering far too much, for far too long."

He began praying over her back and after a moment revealed, "Your bones are fused together. I can feel the bones beginning to separate in your spine."

This woman was noticeably in a lot of pain. The doctor was cradling her compassionately, attempting to soothe her anguish. He whispered, "Yes, I know," in a soft, hushed voice.

This determined but frail woman was now crying. We were seated in the first row of chairs that were directly behind her, watching and listening. All at once, we heard cracking and popping noises. These sounds were clearly coming from her back. Emily and I exchanged looks of disbelief. We silently mouthed words to each other, asking if the other was able to hear the same bursts of snapping sounds emanating from her back.

The sound mimicked popcorn being made in a microwave. Every ten to thirty seconds or so, we would hear another "pop." As each one came, this woman would let out a short but distinct cry. I wasn't sure if her shrieking was due to the discomfort from her bones cracking, the astonishment of what was taking place from within her body, or perhaps a little bit of both. Emily and I continually gave looks of shock back and forth to one another as the popping continued.

Dr. Nemeh told this dear woman that her spine was still moving and asked her if she could feel it. She nodded her head indicating that yes, she most definitely could feel it. He subsequently asked her if it was too much for her, and if so, he promised to stop.

She cried, "No. Please. Don't stop."

While Dr. Nemeh continued to pray, the woman's son was overwhelmed with emotion and was barely able to remain standing. His hands were covering his eyes while trying to stay there next to his mother. Watching his reaction to his mother's experience was equally heartwarming to observe. We were becoming teary-eyed ourselves at the hope and determination coming from this woman and the love of her son. Dr. Nemeh asked the lady to walk around for a few minutes, and as she did, her posture began to change. It went from being severely bent over to standing almost perfectly straight. I checked back over to her son to find he had been so moved in watching his mother's amazing healing that he was now sitting down and sobbing into his hands.

I noticed Nancy wasn't sitting anywhere close by, so I looked around to find her, and I spotted her clear in the back of the room, walking around and stretching her leg probably because of her pain as well as to help prepare for our long ride home. I wondered if she had seen or heard any of what had taken place at the front of the room. After seeing Nancy I was reminded about our upcoming travel with the time constraints and strenuous weather conditions, and decided we had better get moving.

We stood up and headed out of the room where the service was being held, walking out into the hallway where we found Kathy Nemeh. She was sipping on a warm drink and visiting with a few others who were also preparing to leave. Kathy immediately turned toward us to wish us safe travels on our trip back home. Each of the three of us said our goodbyes to Kathy. I was last and thanked her for all she and her husband had done to make this incredible weekend occur. I was astounded by how much I seemed to cherish her, which led me to randomly say that I felt like I had known her my whole life, like she was family. She smiled and hugged me while proclaiming, "We are all family."

She requested we stay in touch with them. Then to my surprise, as we were walking away, she called out, "We will see you again soon."

I wasn't quite sure what she meant by that, but regardless, it made me smile to hear those words from her.

On our way home, I had much to think about while trying to concentrate on driving in unpredictable conditions, as the roads were not the best. We passed so many semitrailers that were jackknifed in the ditches in the first three to four hours of driving that we gave up counting after seeing 25 of them. We had only barely made it into Indiana and had a long way to go yet. Never had I seen so many semis scattered all over the place. It was a mess. I knew I had better try my darndest to focus on the roads to get us home safely. Still, with all the thoughts that were flooding my mind, I found this task nearly impossible.

Nevertheless, I felt entirely secure for some strange reason. It was as if we were being *carried* home somehow, almost celestially, like on the wings of angels. As I became more peaceful while driving, the realization that I hadn't taken any of my medication since my first appointment with Dr. Nemeh on Friday started to hit me. It was now Sunday, and normally, if I had inadvertently missed or skipped even one or two doses, my symptoms typically would begin to come back immediately, and usually with a vengeance. And then, when I would try to start up my medication again, it would normally take weeks or months for my body to correct itself and the medication to work effectively. It was scary to wonder if that predicament could still be a possibility, but all I knew was that I felt better than I had in years. It had me asking myself, *had I really been healed?*

Even though the roads weren't the best, it was a most peaceful drive. As we progressed westward, Nancy and Emily had both become virtually silent. I spiritually felt God's presence and peace with us in the car. The tranquility I felt must have also overcome Nancy, as I noticed her drift off to sleep shortly thereafter. I peered into the rearview mirror to catch a glimpse of what my daughter was doing in the backseat, guessing maybe by now she had fallen asleep too. I was surprised when I saw her wide awake. She appeared to be deep in thought with her eyes gazing out the side window. The look on her face and the expression in her eyes seemed to capture my feelings exactly. I could tell she was doing a lot of soul-searching just from my quick glace in the mirror.

I had countless thoughts racing through my mind such as, *How would I begin to share this entire weekend and all that we had experienced with my husband? And what about my other children? My family? The people I work with?*

In addition to all the miraculous healings that had happened, we had also been taught about the times we are living in and the relevance of our Catholic faith. I thought to myself, *Where would I even begin when telling someone what had happened out there? Some of what had taken place could not even be put into words.* I pondered all these questions in my heart the entire way home.

We pulled into our driveway at a decent time on Sunday evening, and thankfully, we had had no incidents while driving. For me, the time driving had flown by, even though we had pretty much traveled in complete silence. It wasn't that we weren't excited to discuss these topics at greater length; it was more that we were still trying to piece everything together that we had seen, felt, and learned. A vast amount of knowledge and insight had been given in such a short amount of time. I felt as though we had been shown a whole new world.

As the days came and went after returning home to Iowa, my heart was completely transformed. I found myself constantly reflecting on what had happened in that small room in Westlake. Even focusing on tasks at hand became more challenging by the day. I could not imagine how Emily was able to pay close attention and learn in her classes at the university.

Continually reflecting on our time spent in Ohio made me realize that I had had a weight lifted off my shoulders. My soul, for the first time, truly felt renewed and refreshed. I was inspired to take note of everything that had been physically healed or improved since our visit to Ohio, and the list was astounding. All the various emotional and childhood psychological wounds that I had carried around for most of my life were gone as well. I asked myself, *How could I have experienced such a large number of healings, many of which were in so many different areas of my life?*

My soul longed to learn more about the ideas that Dr. Nemeh touched on during those two life-changing days. I had been abundantly filled with love and peace in those moments in that room, especially when I had that magnificent encounter with Jesus. Because of this, I soon found myself yearning for that type of experience to happen again. Emily and I expressed to each other how we wished we could have stayed there and never left. We couldn't help feeling that we wanted to go back, but we knew deep down that wasn't possible.

Over a period of time, I shared my healings with my husband Randy, my three older children – Collette, Josh, and Matt, and my office coworker, Jeannie. Randy was impressed by what had happened to me, and he *wanted* to believe what I told him, but I just don't think he could totally accept it. I understood where he was coming from, how hard it would be for most people to believe, unless they saw it with their own eyes and felt things happen within themselves.

Surprisingly, Jeannie believed what seemed to be every word, at least as much as humanly possible without experiencing it for herself. One day, I told her that I wished I could scoop up everyone I knew and take them to Ohio to encounter God in such a special way for themselves. Most people, myself included, tend not to believe that this kind of healing can happen in today's world, thinking it was only something that took place during the biblical era. But after what happened to me and my daughter, I know for an absolute fact that God has never changed, and He continues to touch the lives of His children today, even through miracles.

In the coming weeks, I noticed my previous ailments continued to disappear, one by one, all while I was still not taking any medication.

Fascinated by this progression, I became curious if my gluten intolerance had disappeared. With so many other miracles taking place, I thought it was worth a try to test it out. Randy initially thought it was an unwise idea. He knew how sick I became if I accidently consumed only a small portion of gluten. This sick feeling would normally consist of periods of severe nausea and a terrible headache that would last for one or more days, leaving me pretty much unable to function.

Even though Dr. Nemeh never mentioned a gluten intolerance healing, and I never said anything to him about it, I still had a strong desire to test for any changes. Once I got up the nerve to try it out, I was thrilled to discover my intolerance was gone. A few days later, I convinced Emily to test her gluten allergy as well, and she had the same miraculous results. The healing of gluten intolerance for both of us was such a nice added surprise, especially since it was nothing we sought after or expected to happen.

What was even more astounding to me was Emily's unwavering faith. She believed from the beginning she had been completely healed from endometriosis. Because of this conviction of hers, she had stopped taking her medication altogether. Since that weekend in January, she has never had any pain or any symptoms of endometriosis again. All the pain in her hips and back she had had before was now entirely gone. She was right. She *had been* healed! It was indeed another miracle!

As I tried to get back into my ordinary way of life, I struggled because I felt differently about everything. I found myself often daydreaming about the deeper meaning of life and the way we spend our time living it. There was a transformation occurring within me with each passing day.

I began to lose interest in worldly things, and my thoughts shifted towards the importance of eternal life.

As I contemplated these daily changes, my health further improved, and I began to cross off several health problems on my initial list, one after the other. Since my rheumatologist scheduled regular occurring appointments for me every three months, I knew I had a checkup appointment coming up in a few short days at the University of Iowa Hospital. Thankfully, most visits were pretty much uneventful. The main purpose of them was to monitor my overall well-being by taking blood and urine samples, and then use the results to monitor autoimmune flare-ups. I gave this upcoming appointment some thought. I wondered if it was worth my time and money to still go. Then I determined that since I felt great, my energy levels were up more with each day, and I wasn't taking any medicine, I would request lab tests a few days in advance of my visit. The results would reveal if there had truly been a change in my health, and after that, I could make an informed decision about keeping my appointment or not.

I sent my doctor a message requesting early testing to reassess my health via the patient portal. My rheumatologist agreed and set it up for me the following day. Since I had completed these lab tests dozens of times, I knew the results would be available in a few short hours. The following day, I drove an hour each way, provided the blood and urine samples needed for testing, came straight home, and without delay, I logged into my medical chart online. Incredibly, I had a notification the tests were complete! I took a deep breath and clicked on the link provided to view the results.

My eyes scanned each line with eager anticipation as the panel of results appeared. Each lab report in the past indicated abnormal results, but for the first time in *years*, there was a drastic shift. Each one of the results were now lying directly in the "normal" range. I read them repeatedly, clicking back and forth, screen to screen, reviewing past findings and now my current results. It took me a while before it sank in, but when it did, I was incredibly grateful.

The reality of it all was more than my emotions could handle. I had a tremendous sense of relief in knowing I had truly experienced a life-saving miracle that weekend in Ohio! I started to cry tears of joy and amazement as I whispered, "How could a disease be erased like that? Oh, thank you, God! Thank you!"

After nearly a half hour had passed, I fixed my eyes back at the computer screen for another minute and printed out the results to show my husband when he came home from work. Randy had visibly noticed the changes in my energy levels and health, but I suspected he was still skeptical that this new change was more from a placebo effect than an honest healing. I doubted that he believed the autoimmune disease had really left. I am not entirely sure I honestly believed it myself before having the proof in front of me. I understood how implausible it seemed that something like this could really happen.

Precisely as he walked through the door that evening, I ran right up to him, giving him a gigantic hug and a kiss "hello," while handing him the results. I smiled and exclaimed, "You need to take a look at these!"

He was attempting to balance his lunch box and our daily mail, while trying to take off his shoes and understand what was going on with me. I could tell he was searching my face in an attempt to figure it all out. Despite the strange stare he was giving me, I kept smiling back at him. I could hardly wait for him to read the report.

He gave me another confused look by raising his eyebrow. He flashed a brief, unusual smile at me indicating how odd he thought I was acting. He finally managed to slip off his brown leather work shoes and put his lunchbox with the pile of mail down. He then proceeded to pull up a barstool to our kitchen island. He sat down, attempting to focus his mind and eyes on what I had handed him. Before he took a good look, he glanced back up at me with a puzzled expression and asked, "Christy, what is this all about?"

"Come on, Randy. Please read it!" I begged, beaming with excitement.

He surveyed the papers quickly and then glanced right back up at me, showing that same confused state he was in only seconds earlier. I could tell he was not putting the pieces together yet.

"Randy, please read it." I pleaded.

"These are my test results from the doctor today. I went there this morning and had them retest me. Each one of them is *completely* normal since returning from Ohio!"

I knew this would be such a huge turning point for Randy. He is an engineer and numbers are essential to him. It was visible proof to the fact that I had most definitely received a miracle. He may have been able to explain away my lack of symptoms as a coincidence or short-term anomaly, but seeing tangible medical results was not as easy to dismiss.

Even I had doubts. I often wondered if I only *thought* I was healed. I am not sure why I would have reservations about any of it after everything that I had experienced that weekend. In my heart, I knew the lack of complete trust in what I was shown was disgraceful. Little did I know, God had a plan to educate me in how to surrender and trust more in the upcoming months ahead. And goodness knows, I surely needed all the lessons God could give me!

That entire evening, Randy and I continued to discuss the meaning of my test results. It took a while, but I could tell he began to understand what had truly happened. I could almost see the wheels spinning in his head while he was thinking. The next day, once he appeared to fully grasp the situation at hand, he turned to me and asked what this meant for me and my health in the future. I told him, "Well, I sure don't think I need to go see my rheumatologist anymore, and I'm canceling my upcoming Mayo Clinic appointment as well."

We both laughed at such an obvious statement. Ironically, a few days passed and my rheumatologist dismissed me from her care because I no longer displayed any signs of autoimmune health problems. The amount of joy this created in me was equal to the gratitude my heart found with each new day.

Mark 11:24 (NRSV)
So I tell you, whatever you ask for in prayer,
believe that you have received it, and it will be yours.

eight.

Mother Daughter Miracles

DAYS WERE ROLLING BY since our life-changing visit to Ohio, which encouraged me to seriously reflect on what transpired in that special treatment room, as well as revaluate what really took place back in 2011. Finally, eight years later, I began to connect the dots from my very first prayer with Dr. Nemeh, the one that literally knocked me off my feet. I understood that a miracle had taken place at that exact moment, and I finally made the connection between my healing and my cardiologist's statement that I had had a "misdiagnosis."

I questioned myself, *How I could have been so blind?* I was really blown away at my own ignorance. Somehow back then, I never examined what had happened. I was completely in the dark to God's mercy that had kept me from needing a serious operation, heart surgery. Thankfully, I was given a second chance to discover the truth. This time around, I was able to see God's hand in all of it and have the opportunity to share what had happened with others.

Randy and Emily were the only two people with whom I fully shared my encounter with Jesus and the rest of our experience in Dr. Nemeh's office. Everything that had taken place seemed very personal and challenging when I tried to describe it to others. When I began to share some of my experiences with family, friends, and strangers, I feared they would think I was crazy. Instead of only sharing my personal healings and journey, I started to lend out the book, Miracles Every Day, to anyone interested in learning more about Dr. Nemeh, his faith, and the reality that God is always walking with us.

As people were continuously being enlightened by the book, Emily and I stumbled upon an incredibly powerful podcast series called *Blind Faith Live*. This series was produced from 2013 to 2017. Dr. Nemeh, Kathy Nemeh, and hundreds of people with miraculous healing stories were interviewed in the podcasts. The people being interviewed would describe what had happened to them after receiving a prayer from Dr. Nemeh.

Once Emily and I began listening to the podcasts, we were hooked. It felt like we had just struck a spiritual gold mine. All of the topics discussed in these podcasts presented important information regarding the nature of our spirituality and how we are truly called to live according to Christ's teaching. The messages were so impactful that we would listen for hours at a time, trying to soak up as much knowledge as humanly possible.

On Friday afternoons, Emily would drive an hour from college to spend the weekend with her father and me at home. We spent much of our time listening to these podcasts and journaling about what we had learned. I absolutely cherished these moments we spent together, and I realize now they were very instrumental in helping us come to understand the refining that was taking place within ourselves. We felt that we were being drawn closer and closer to God each day, as if He were spiritually preparing us for something in the future.

We knew that before our time with Dr. Nemeh, we had both loved God, but regrettably, He was not the complete center of our lives. Now it was as if our souls had been ignited with the fire of the Holy Spirit, and we thought of Him continuously. Living this way was such a blessing, but it also came with many hardships. We no longer held many of our previous interests. The time spent having meaningless conversations, watching television, etc. seemed senseless now. It was like we had been reprogrammed, wishing to only use our time to center our minds around God and helping others.

Life seemed to be rushing by and it wasn't long before Emily would be on spring break. Thankfully, I was able to take a week off work to spend one-on-one time with Emily during her spring vacation. Our love for Christ had deepened so much since our trip to Ohio that we were looking for more ways to include Him in our everyday lives. During Emily's spring break, the two of us decided to find and attend a weekday Mass. Our local parish didn't offer this, so we found a nearby church (Immaculate Conception) in a neighboring town (Cedar Rapids) that offered daily Mass. It was a forty-minute drive from our home, but because our longing to attend Mass was so great, we didn't think twice about driving the distance to get there.

It was a weekday, and we were pleasantly surprised at the number of people in attendance on a weekday. I expected there would only have been a handful of people, but it was filled, and with people of all ages, even some with young families. The church itself appeared unique somehow, like it had an added element of holiness to it. The priest who celebrated mass also seemed extraordinary. I didn't know who he was at the time, but his reverence was quite refreshing and inspirational. This church truly had a way of making the light of Christ shine and sparked a flame in us so intense that we desired to come back again, and we did. Again. And again. We attended daily Mass every day, all week long.

Our week together was full of simple but spiritual activities. Our days consisted of attending daily Mass, studying faith-related topics, reading about saints and the remarkable lives they led, and listening to podcasts. I acquired more knowledge about my faith during those few days than I had in the last twenty years put together.

The entire week was unlike any other, and before I knew it, it was time for Emily to return to school and for me to go back to work. We weren't saddened by this; in fact, we were both joyful and felt a closeness with God that neither of us had ever known before. At times, we could actually *feel* Jesus walking among us. It gave us both such a tremendous sense of peace.

As we went back to our normal activities of school and work, I recalled that both Kathy and Dr. Nemeh had asked us to stay in touch and keep them posted of how our healings progressed. I sat down and wrote a letter of appreciation to them, sharing some of what had transpired since our visit.

My letter to the Nemehs on March 17, 2019:

Dear Dr. & Kathy Nemeh,

Last month, on January 18th, my daughter, my co-worker, and I drove from Iowa to come there for a couple of medical appointments with Dr. Nemeh and we arrived before a bad snowstorm had hit. I had two appointments scheduled with him: one that Friday night we got in and the other was the first appointment of the day on Saturday. My daughter, Emily, and my co-worker, Nancy, both joined in on the appointments and then all three of us had a ticket for the prayer service on Sunday.

I am writing as both of you had asked us, ever so kindly, to stay in touch. We have so much goodness to share from what we have experienced, but I won't be able to write you about everything as I know how precious your time is and when I had explained some of our story to family members it took several hours. I will try to keep this short and sweet.

First let me say, how extremely thankful we are for the both of you! We have shared our experience with many people and have loaned out our two copies of "Miracles Every Day" to multiple people, even before coming. The visit we had there was life changing for my daughter and I for so many reasons. The most important thing that has occurred is I feel like my heart was pierced during my appointment and nothing has been the same for me since. Emily, my daughter, who is nineteen years old has mentioned having the same experience.

Dr. Nemeh spent so much time with us the first night that it was after 1:00 a.m. before he went home. Not only did he treat me with his acupuncture and such, but the prayers he said were not only for me, BUT he also took the time to pray for my co-worker and my daughter. It was such a touching experience and both visits were incredibly moving!

The second morning, near the end of my visit, he shared with us a vision he had in 2018 about the Second Coming and things happening in the Church. I bet he spoke for nearly forty-five minutes about issues that we had already had concerns and wonderings about before our visit, all the while continuing to work as he spoke. At times you could hear the urgency in his words.

We have had so many physical healings, both my daughter and I. I will name the big ones:

My daughter's endometriosis seems to have subsided or perhaps completely disappeared and she also has stopped taking her medication. Her back is straighter and feels so much better.

I stopped all medication for lupus and have felt great! At the same time, I have had absolutely no symptoms for fibromyalgia or Raynaud's Syndrome either. Instead of wearing my gloves in this crazy cold weather, a lot of times I just carry them around as not having any pain in the cold has been so wonderful!

I have only had one migraine since I have gotten back which is amazing for me (normally I have eight or so a month). Also, a week or so after being home all my neck and hand pain from arthritis has completely left. My back-arthritis pain too has been feeling like it is continuing to lift. We are both eternally grateful for having been able to come there and have this opportunity to meet you all in person and being able to talk and discuss such important things. It has made our hearts so, so happy!

After returning home, I think both our hearts were left there in Ohio somewhere. It is hard to explain, but it was like a deep loss. We both felt such a profound connection to both of you. I mentioned to Kathy at the healing service I felt like we had just found our long, lost relatives and she reminded me we are all related. You both have been placed in our hearts forever and my daughter and I both pray for you guys every single day.

One more thing I would like to mention, since coming home, we so luckily stumbled onto the Issam's Insights on "Blind Faith Live" as well as the Miracle Moments and Keeping It Real with Kathy! We are hooked and learning so much from Dr. Nemeh & absolutely love hearing from Kathy, too. She is very spunky, and we love her spirit!

Emily is back at the University of Northern Iowa now but we both listen on our own to the podcasts & even take notes. When we see each other on the weekends we share what we are learning. Emily has felt since she was a little girl that we are in the End Times and has told me several times she thought it would be during her lifetime…she had told me these things before I had ever really given it a lot of thought. She is very "connected" as Dr. Nemeh puts it and has had some very special events in her life with angels and other unique experiences that a person just can't explain other than God reaching into her life. I have seen so many things happening in recent years that I too do not doubt "we are in it," the End Times that is.

We have been very busy sharing what has happened there in Ohio for us and the thousands of other miracles you all have had by again telling others about the book and now also the podcasts.

Our lives will NEVER be the same and this is most definitely a good thing but at the same time it is a bit difficult. At times, each one of us feels like we just don't fit in as well anymore. I think both of us have always been different than the mainstream, but this has been a more profound change that others can see, and I sense recently are wondering what happened to us. Neither one of us is no longer worried what someone will think of when we choose to do something or not…now we both are only concerned with what God will think.

Also, one thing that has stuck with me is how Dr. Nemeh shared how he is so connected to Jesus he isn't scared of anything…then looked right at me and repeated, "Nothing!" I felt like that message was for me personally and is something I will always remember.

I don't know how you thank two people for changing our lives in so many beautiful ways. I wished we lived closer to participate or help with your ministry in one way or another as I know we would both drop anything and be there in an instant. We have both shared with each other that we wished we lived there now for these reasons. If there is ever anything we can do for you, please let us know. We are willing to do anything we can to help others get connected to God as well. We will continue sharing and hopefully sending others your way for more healings.... especially of people's hearts/minds.

Take care and may God bless you both for all you do for God and for others! You have truly blessed our lives in more ways than I could ever express. I have put all of your healing services on our calendar and if we can get out there again, we will.....and hopefully bring some more family members & friends with us.

Many Blessings,

Christy Blake

PS—We have also both discovered that since being back our gluten intolerance also has left! That was a very fun discovery!!

As the days and weeks came and went, I continued to marvel at the changes in my daughter and me. I remembered my past comment to Jeannie, how I wished I could rent a bus to take everyone to Ohio. I wanted people to know that what had happened to us was also possible for them. It was something I said quite often. The idea was so compelling that it flowed straight from my heart and into my words more and more.

At the time, I never dreamed any of it would become a reality, nor did I realize that God had "bigger plans." Little did I know, He had mysteriously planted this tiny seed of an idea straight into my soul, and slowly, with each day, He began to nurture it, causing it to become bigger and stronger.

My mind became more preoccupied with it all the time. I began to imagine people with various medical issues hearing about what had happened to us and then being inspired to come on a bus trip to experience the power of God for themselves. A small part of me must have known there was a possibility that it could really happen, because I began calculating that if this was going to come true, I should actually begin planning for it by putting some money aside. So, without telling anyone, not even my husband, I began to do just that. From that point on, I took every one of my paychecks and placed them into a separate savings account. I never researched how to put this idea into motion, nor did I know how much it would cost. All I knew was if this was really going to take place, I wanted to pay half of the cost of the trip in order to make it affordable for whoever may come.

With each passing day, I began to think about it more and more. I was even having dreams about it. I finally had to do something since I couldn't keep it to myself any longer. On April 9, I finally gave in and decided to write an email to Kathy Nemeh, letting her know what was in my heart, asking what she and the doctor thought about it. As I stared at my computer screen, I tried to find the words and the courage to write, but I became extremely nervous and started having reservations about it. I began to change my mind about the whole idea, thinking it was probably unrealistic and just plain silly. As I was about to give up, an email suddenly flowed straight across my screen and into my inbox right before my eyes. The email came from *Path to Faith*.

Path to Faith is the organization affiliated with Dr. and Kathy Nemeh's healing services. I knew this email wasn't only being sent to me; it was an electronic message that is generated several times a year with updates and miracle stories. They send it to a wide list, including all the past healing service participants.

This email, however, contained something that took me by surprise. The newest highlighted miracle story they featured was called "Mother – Daughter Miracles," and unexpectedly, it was my own. It contained the same letter I had written to them just one month earlier. I froze. I knew right then that the timing of the Nemeh's email at that precise moment, when I was feeling such hesitation to write to them, was no coincidence. This was a sign given straight from Heaven to persevere in writing my email to Kathy. Little did I know, this was only the beginning of many blessings, signs, and wonders to come. Once I truly surrendered to God, nothing has ever been the same.

Psalm 9:2 (NRSV)
I will be glad and exult in You;
I will sing praise to Your name, O Most High.

nine.

Leap of Faith

GOD'S TIMING IS ALWAYS perfect. I hadn't moved an inch since receiving and reading the email from *Path to Faith* with our miracle story being showcased. The email came through just in the nick of time, preventing me from abandoning my dream. It encouraged me to push forward with this beautiful mission that God had placed in my heart. I took a deep breath and began to write to Kathy.

My original email to Kathy Nemeh on April 9, 2019:

Dear Kathy,

I received your email from the "Path to Faith Organization" this morning and it was totally God's timing. First of all, I want to say thank you so much for placing our Mother/Daughter Story in there that I sent you not too long ago. That was a very beautiful thing to do! And secondly, I have been meaning to email you about a thought that has been on my heart for the last several months, so again, the timing of that email this morning made me smile.

Since we have left there and have been sharing our story of what transpired with me, Emily, and one of my co-workers, Nancy, I cannot get it out of my head that everyone should be able to experience what we did during those three days. One of my coworkers, who didn't go with us, Jeannie, completely believes in the same idea and we know so many people who would truly benefit in going there to attend a healing service. Jeannie has been helping me share about you and we have several new people listening to the podcasts now!

Since sharing my story with her, I briefly mentioned that we should rent a charter bus and take people out to see you guys for one of your healing services. Jeannie completely agrees with me. But other than saying that aloud, no more has happened since...except, I cannot get this idea out my head and heart!

I feel like God planted this whole idea Himself. I am even dreaming about it! At one point I thought perhaps it was me that was overly thinking about it and trying to push it. Then, I thought I should let God move matters and keep quiet. Well, that lasted less than one day as the feeling is so strong, I can't keep it to myself.

I had told myself and my daughter, Emily, that I would email you this week to see what you guys thought of this and if you had a date on the calendar that you would like us to use and shoot for, or perhaps you would like to use a different day that is not already scheduled? We are hoping it would bring around fifty people as I think that is about how many would fit on a charter bus, but it is hard to know how many would actually sign up for it. I know many people do not have the opportunity to drive that far or fly so if we offered the transportation, and being in the community of others, that perhaps this would be an amazing opportunity for people.

I wanted to pick up the phone to call you and discuss but sometimes big ideas like this take some time to ponder and think about, so I thought sending you an email would be the best idea. Plus, I tend to do better with writing matters out than speaking. I would like both of your opinions, and anyone else that would be involved.

I am at work today. Perhaps you could email me back with a good day and time and I could call you back? Or you could call me? If you don't think the timing is right that is okay, I know how busy you both are and still am so completely touched by the lives you both live. I still cannot believe how much my thoughts, my life, my everything has changed since being there.

I hope to hear back from you soon. I cannot thank you all enough for what you have done for our lives, health, hearts...and our spirits. We will be forever grateful and hoping this would allow me to give you a little bit of thank you to you both... and to God as well.

Have a beautiful day!

Her response was short and sweet.
Email from Kathy on April 9, 2019:

Hi Christy,

This is totally amazing! Please call me anytime. My cell phone number is (440) xxx-xxxx.

Many blessings
Kathy

I called Kathy as quickly as I could. She seemed thrilled about all of it and said that they would be willing to work with Emily and me to make this work. I could hardly believe this was happening! Given that I needed a little time to figure out where to go from here, I requested a few days to get things in order first, and then I would get back to her.

My head was spinning! I was so excited! I felt more enthusiasm about doing this than anything else I had ever done in my entire life! I knew this idea of taking a busload of people to Ohio for a healing service with Dr. Nemeh could be so powerful and life-changing for others.

Before I could move forward in planning, I knew I had to consult my supervisor at work and my husband. I loved my job as a faith formation coordinator, but there were some circumstances at work that were causing me to consider resigning. More importantly at home, I still had to talk with my husband about this whole idea. Randy is a very loving and thoughtful person; however, money can be a rather challenging subject to discuss with him. He tends to think I am overly generous when it comes to spending, and he, in contrast, is a saver. He doesn't like to spend money period. For me to tell him that I had this desire to organize a bus trip, let alone offer to pay half of the bus expense myself, was a huge, scary step. I wanted him on board with my proposal, and I couldn't see myself fulfilling this dream without his blessing and support.

I decided to tackle the obstacle with my husband first. Emily was on fire with the entire plan and was prepared to offer her assistance in any way possible to help make this event a reality. She knew my concerns with her father and how I was terribly worried that he would find this entire idea to be outrageous.

Emily and I decided to pray about how we should approach this issue with Randy. Our prayers were heard, and we were given the idea of starting a "novena." A novena is a very powerful prayer that is prayed every day for nine consecutive days. Even though we are Catholic, neither one of us knew much about them. After doing some research, I discovered the very first novena was believed to have started with the Blessed Mother and Jesus' disciples when they spent nine days in prayer together between the Ascension and Pentecost.

We were led to the perfect novena which invoked the prayers of St. Padre Pio, who was well known for his charity and piety. Emily and I promised one another we would each pray for the following nine days, imploring Jesus to soften Randy's heart. As we prayed, amazing things began taking place, even during the first few days.

Each day when Randy would be close to arriving home from work, or seconds before he would call me on the phone, I would experience a pleasant but strong scent, wafting towards me in the air. There was no mistaking it, and the aroma smelled like flowers, specifically the fragrance of lilies. It was like a small glimpse of Heaven, or perhaps I should say a *smell* of Heaven. Emily understood that this was a sign that St. Padre Pio was present and that our prayers for Randy were being heard and answered.

When our novena was complete, we nervously sat Randy down to discuss our hopes and plans. We explained that we wanted to take people to Ohio for one of Dr. Nemeh's healing prayer services so that others could see and feel the power of God, just like we had. To do this, we would need to rent a charter bus, and I also wanted to make it affordable by paying half the cost of the bus. His unbelievable response to my request, even with a smile, was simply, "Okay."

Emily and I stared at each other in disbelief to Randy's reply. A smile swept across both of our faces at the sheer amazement of what had just taken place! If anyone knew my husband, they would know that Randy's green light and cooperation were for sure a miracle! I had no doubt that our prayers, along with St. Padre Pio's intercession, helped Randy to trust and support our plans. I could hardly believe it! It was really going to happen!

My next task was to resolve my problems with work, if possible. This toxic situation was constantly on my mind, which led me to prayer, and eventually directed me to reach out to Kathy Nemeh for some guidance. Naturally, she gave me the best advice ever, with such a simple and profound message saying, "You need to get out of there. You will soar!"

After reading this email, over and over, praying, and discussing this in detail with my family, I decided to listen to her advice and take a leap of faith by giving my two-week notice. My last day of work was April 30, 2019. Once I had officially left work, I reached back out to Kathy, explaining how I had taken her advice to heart and resigned from my position. It was like a breath of fresh air. I was now prepared to move forward and begin working on the bus trip full time.

I originally thought we would most likely be attending another healing service that the Nemehs had previously scheduled. However, much to my surprise, Kathy told me she had spoken to her husband, and they wished to offer us our own private day! I was stunned by their incredible generosity!

It almost seemed too good to be true, as if it were all a dream. We picked out the date together, and the healing service was scheduled to be held on Saturday, May 25, 2019. This particular day fell right over Memorial Day weekend. I began trembling with excitement and could hardly wait to call Emily and tell her the wonderful news!

Kathy graciously helped us in every manner possible. She traveled around Ohio searching for the perfect place for our special day. She came across a Catholic Retreat Center that they thought would best suit the healing prayer service. She was beyond kind in showing us the location by forwarding photos and videos of the place to be sure we thought it seemed suitable. Of course we thought it was lovely and would be a beautiful, prayerful location.

Kathy generously went to great lengths to make our event even more special. She not only lined up the retreat center, but she also graciously arranged to take care of lunch for our entire group. Additionally, she helped coordinate our stay by providing phone numbers to local hotels in Ohio and offering her guidance and support throughout the process.

The next step was reserving the charter bus. I had to do some research because I really had no clue on how to go about renting a bus, but it didn't take long. I found several websites that offered direction, and I lined one up in no time.

Last but not least, we needed a name for our trip and a website. Emily and I sat together jotting down names we believed would contain the perfect God-inspired title revealing the main idea behind the trip. Nearly an hour and many failed suggestions later, Emily jumped up and called out, "I've got it! The Blessed Reason Trip!"

She elaborated, "Mom, don't you remember when you said you didn't think you should be there with Dr. Nemeh in January? And then he told you, 'You are here for *a blessed reason*?'"

We intuitively knew *this* was the reason, to help bring healing to others, and would also be the name of our trip! The title also held a strong message that God calls each one of us for a "blessed reason," and it is our responsibility to share our experiences and the "Good News" with others. From that point forward, we used the name, *The Blessed Reason Trip.*

After we decided what to call the trip, we designed a website that presented details about the upcoming weekend retreat, information on

Dr. Nemeh, and our own story. We also provided links to news reports documenting healing stories involving Dr. Nemeh, including his appearance on *The Dr. Oz Show* that I had watched in 2011. This website gave people the chance to conduct their own research on Dr. Nemeh and the specifics regarding our trip before officially signing up. Emily and I also designed flyers and postcards that we could hand out to people so they could take the information home and read more about it.

All the details came together flawlessly. It had only been three days since making the commitment to offer this trip, and we had everything arranged. Looking back, it's astonishing to see how fast it all came together. God truly guided us along every step of the way. Considering we had only four weeks before the trip to Ohio, and no one had signed up yet, I began to brainstorm ideas on how to reach the "right" people. Unfortunately, this didn't come easy for me, and I still had many difficult lessons to learn about surrendering and trusting God.

As I was striving to think of the best way to reach the "right" people, I came up with an idea to distribute the postcards and flyers in parking ramps of nearby hospitals. It seemed like such a perfect way to reach those who could be ill or searching for healing. Emily and I drove to several different hospitals in neighboring towns, walking many miles and devoting countless hours to place our information on people's windshields. We were committed to this new mission of ours, but we were devastated when one week later, not one person had responded.

Randy sensed my disappointment and lack of confidence that this trip could go any further and asked if it were possible to get our money back on the bus rental. I hadn't even checked if that were an option; I had only written the check for the full amount and simply trusted God. At this point, I was having serious doubts about all of it and was becoming increasingly worried with each passing day.

The number of people we had signed up for the trip had not changed. It was still at zero. I knew this trip had the possibility of being a life-changing opportunity for many people, but it felt like we had hit a brick wall and I didn't know where to turn. With much sadness in my heart, I emailed Kathy to share my frustrations in how I was struggling with this project and ask if she had any advice for me. She simply assured me that if I was indeed following God's lead, it would all work out perfectly.

Her short and sweet reply made me question, *was I **truly** following God's lead? Was I praying for God's guidance on what to do and how to make it all work? Or was I only moving forward with what I thought would work, never even thinking to ask God how **He** wanted me to do it?*

It didn't take long for me to figure out that I had gone about this process all wrong. Not one time had I asked God to show me the way. I was praying, but only to be successful in the way that I chose, asking God to bless *my* ways. My prayers hadn't been fruitful because of my approach. It never occurred to me to seek how God wanted me to proceed with each step until Kathy so beautifully brought this idea to light.

When this message sank in, I began to reflect on the ways God had tried to gain my attention in the past. I noticed how once I had gotten the go ahead and the details arranged for the trip, I moved full speed ahead, using my own ideas, without ever stopping to seek or to be inspired. I certainly wasn't spending much time in silence or paying attention to signs being given to me either. For example, one day my husband suggested that we should create a Facebook page. I dismissed the idea right away, thinking that wasn't the best way to proceed for a private healing service. I had never thought to pray about it or recognize that God could be speaking through my husband. I admit part of the reason I dismissed him was because I was scared. The not-so-distant memories of how I had lost relationships due to my newfound love for God frightened me and kept me from placing this event on social media for everyone to see. When I finally thought this through, it hit me, *why did I care what others thought anyway? Wasn't I supposed to be living for God? Isn't that what really mattered?*

Without delay, Emily and I sat down together at our dining room table and created our Blessed Reason Trip Facebook page. That was such a huge learning moment for me, and it taught me to always turn my eyes and ears more towards God, asking him to lead the way – to pray and then *wait* on the Lord to answer in every situation. I was so appreciative for Kathy's wisdom and guidance which led me to question if I was truly seeking God's direction or my own.

John 5:30 (NRSV)
"I can do nothing on my own. As I hear, I judge; and my judgment is just, because I seek to do not my own will but the will of Him who sent me."

ten.

Waiting on the Lord

THERE IS A SAYING that I have heard in the past: "People say to God, show me, and I will believe, but God says, believe, and I will show you!"

This expression seemed to come to life the moment that I decided to stop being the one in control - and instead surrender, trust, and follow God. When I finally believed God would guide me, He definitely showed me! A few days later, following the adaptation of my new approach, something incredible happened. When I was out driving and not thinking of anything in particular, I suddenly heard two distinct names. Like a flash, I had an awareness that these two names, independent of one another, were sent to me for a special purpose. I knew they would somehow help me find the individuals that God intended to come on the bus trip. However, I had two main concerns: first, I had no idea who these people were exactly, and second, I didn't know how they would be involved.

I pulled over and wrote both names down in my phone. When I got home, I researched who they were. One name belonged to a priest in nearby Cedar Rapids, Iowa. I soon figured out that this was the priest who was pastor of the parish we were led to back in March - Immaculate Conception Catholic Church. He was the same priest that Emily and I had both found to be incredibly reverent. I never knew his name or anything about him before this day, so I was quite shocked by this fact. I understood that God had arranged for us to be directed to this parish and priest for a much greater purpose.

The other God-given name belonged to a cofounder of a Regional Catholic Conference in Des Moines, Iowa. Her name is Ellen Miller. Most Catholics who live in the state of Iowa know who she is. I certainly recognized her name, but I didn't know her personally, nor did I have the faintest idea how she would be able to help me, especially since she lived two hours away. All I knew was that God had a plan.

I knew I was meant to contact both of these individuals; I chose to reach out to the local priest in Cedar Rapids first. I found his email address online and sent him a message explaining who I was, the circumstances regarding our healing stories, and why I felt called to organize this bus trip because of it. I also gave him a brief background of how his name had been placed into my heart for assistance in helping us spread the word. His response was very kind, "I would be happy to help you."

I knew his name had been furnished for a special purpose, but I was still surprised at how smooth it went. After our correspondence, I gave him more information and told him we were short on time to find those meant to go. He generously allowed us to place our postcards and flyers inside his parish and place an announcement in the church bulletin. It was very heartwarming to have him team up with us for such a powerful mission.

Next, I sought a way to contact Ellen, the other person whose name God had given me. I found the *Christ Our Life* Facebook page and sent her a private message, leaving my contact information. This incredible faith-filled woman called me up right away. I relayed my story to her, including how God had sent me her name, and to my amazement, she was incredibly supportive of our cause. I told her I was confused that God had given me her name, wondering how she could help being that she lived so far away. Ellen laughed and reassured me that she knew exactly how she could help. She mentioned that she was affiliated with religious organizations in the Cedar Rapids area, which allowed her to connect with some of those people and ask if they would be willing to be of assistance. Ellen was incredibly thoughtful and helpful in every possible way.

That same evening, my phone was ringing off the hook with people she knew offering to help us in a number of ways. They provided us with dates and locations of upcoming events, encouraging Emily and I to attend and share this important mission with others. It was unbelievable how quick the word spread, not to mention the amount of love and generosity we were shown by strangers who had been touched by our story and wanted to share God's goodness with their community.

Throughout the next few weeks, our lives were a complete whirlwind. Emily and I attended one event after another, announcing the details about our bus trip. This of course always culminated with us sharing our own stories. It was a new, exciting world for both of us, but it also took us out of our comfort zones. Due to the numerous events and the small amount of time we had to reach people, we were rarely home. Most days, we would not get back to the house until well after ten o'clock at night. I suspected my husband was most likely questioning what in the world we had signed up for because it took over almost every aspect of our lives.

When we went to church functions or gatherings, we would be sure to make the case that this was God's trip, and not ours. God inspired this whole idea in my heart, and being so, I knew He must have determined in advance who He would inspire to go with us to Ohio. After learning such a valuable lesson about how doing things on our own hadn't worked out too well, we became more prayerful in our approach from that point forward.

With only two more weeks before our trip, we definitely started seeing the fruit from our surrender to God's will. We now had thirty-one people signed up. Even so, my husband who had agreed in the beginning to allow us to host this event, was now beginning to waver about the trip. He was starting to calculate how much it would *truly* cost us. He knew that if we only had thirty-one people, this also meant we had twenty-five empty seats. The numbers indicated we would, in all reality, be spending a lot more than I had originally calculated.

I could see how incredibly hard this was for him to trust that it would all work out. I was being given signs left and right and so was Emily, but Randy, on the other hand, was just left with my promise that this was meant to be.

Thankfully, one day, I was inspired to reveal to Randy some of what was happening with Emily and me. I also was quick to remind him of where this idea had come from in the first place. I could not believe how easy it was for us to sometimes forget who was in control. Occasionally, when there were trials, even after everything I had been shown, I still struggled to completely trust God through it. At times, I felt quite ashamed at my own lack of faith even though the lessons God had taught me proved, over and over again, that I could trust Him. I had to be patient and wait for His timing and not try to figure things out on my own using human logic. He had a more perfect plan. Reaching out to Randy that day helped reassure him that sponsoring this trip was the right thing to do.

The Holy Spirit used all sorts of techniques to guide me such as providing names and/or mental pictures of individuals, vivid dreams, a sudden smell of roses, a burning or a literal tug on my heart, similar to the first time we had met Dr. Nemeh. The sensations weren't only happening to me; they were also occurring with Emily too. Each of them was highly effective in guiding us to the right people and using the right words as we spoke to them.

Usually when we were inspired to approach someone, the individual would express their interest and gratitude to us for reaching out to them. Based on people's reactions, we could see right away whether we were truly following God's promptings on who to ask, or if we were acting on our own. The difference in their responses said it all and helped keep us steady in prayer and concentrating on where we would be guided next.

Occasionally, we would come across people who longed to go, but they sadly thought they didn't deserve to be healed, that they were somehow unworthy to ask God to heal them. This was the same way I had initially felt back when I sat in Dr. Nemeh's office. In this past year, I have learned through Dr. Nemeh, that we are ALL worthy. God *does* desire that we ask, seek, and knock.

As the days went by, we had several people cancel their ticket due to their own unbelief or misgivings. It was disheartening, especially if this happened with a person we knew had a serious issue, someone we felt God was specifically *calling* to be with us. The most we could do in those situations was to tell them how strongly we felt they were meant to come with us. We simply were unable to explain *how* we knew that God was calling them to come. My goodness, neither Emily nor I could entirely understand what was happening to us with the multiple signs we were so miraculously being given, let alone try to speak about it to someone we barely knew. We still had so much to learn.

There were many times I would cry, tormented in knowing a particular person should go. I could only sit back and pray, waiting for them to decide on their own. It was very difficult. It may sound strange to hear that we would be shedding tears for complete strangers, but these people and their needs were by some mysterious and wonderful way, directly written onto our hearts. Our thoughts and prayers were heavily invested in those who were meant to be with us.

Waiting for the prayers to be answered was the most challenging task of this undertaking. We were learning through each day to trust that we would be led to the people God willed to go. They, in turn, somehow received the courage to trust that our intentions were genuine, coming from our love for God and others. I have no doubt that this came from prayers being answered.

However, I did have days where my prayers were filled with sorrow and anguish due to the many empty bus seats we had yet to fill. Having empty seats seemed so sad to me because of the huge potential that each one carried. I was quickly reminded that even one person receiving a healing would be well worth my efforts. I had to keep in complete accordance with God's will and not my own. Perhaps it was not meant to be a full bus.

Eventually, we ended up having a total of forty-three people sign up for our blessed trip! Throughout this stretch of time, God repeatedly answered our prayers and blessed our lives with more than we could ever deserve. We had no idea that God would continue to bless us with a sense of community, friendship, and family with those who had signed up for the Blessed Reason Trip. It sure wasn't an easy road, but it was worth every trial we had to face to experience the power and beauty of following God's unwavering hand.

Proverbs 3:5-6 (NRSV)
Trust in the Lord with all your heart,
and do not rely on your own insight.
In all your ways acknowledge Him,
and He will make straight your paths.

eleven.

Pilgrims on a Journey

THE DAY WE HAD all been waiting for finally arrived. Emily and I welcomed everyone, introduced ourselves, as well as my husband Randy and our two sons, Josh and Matt. We loaded the charter bus full of people, luggage, and snacks, and prayed as a group for our special weekend together and safe travels. As we placed our trip in God's Hands, we departed for Ohio in hopes of renewal, healing, and growth.

During the bus ride, Emily and I gave a detailed account of our own healings to the whole group. We knew most were aware that we had had some healings, but nobody, besides our family, knew our story. We felt it was important to share our testimony to help people understand who we were, who Dr. Nemeh was, and how God had touched our lives. I described some of the miracles we had experienced and conveyed that God had a plan for each one of them too.

After introducing ourselves and our stories, we offered to anyone interested in learning more about Dr. Nemeh and how he has dedicated his entire life to Jesus the chance to read the book *Miracles Every Day*. We had brought several copies with us. Several people took advantage of the opportunity and told me how thankful they were. This book is such an eye opener for people wanting to understand just how connected Dr. Nemeh is with the Holy Spirit. A few people chose to read the book after the trip, only to tell me they wished they had read it before they were in front of him, because it would have helped them appreciate and respect Dr. Nemeh's faith even more.

Emily and I each made our way through the bus, talking with people individually, as well as listening to their stories and reasons for coming on this trip. We shared what we had learned about ourselves, our faith in God, and even about Dr. Nemeh. They were all so kind to us, and I was humbled to be a part of their search for healing. We kept busy visiting with each person to ensure everyone was comfortable.

We made a stop for food and bathroom breaks nearly every two hours. My husband and two sons were very kind and graciously offered everyone snacks and drinks during each stop. They were the three perfect gentlemen and made all of the guests feel welcome.

With all of our stops, I found out the hard way that a normal nine-hour car drive magically turns into a twelve-hour bus ride. I hadn't considered that having forty-three people getting on and off the bus for breaks could drastically increase our overall time on the road. We left Cedar Rapids, Iowa at two o'clock in the afternoon on Friday, and didn't reach Westlake, Ohio until two o'clock in the morning on Saturday.

Luckily, our healing service didn't begin until 11:00 a.m., allowing our passengers to get *some* sleep.

By the time we finally arrived at the hotel, everyone was completely exhausted. Regrettably, the hotel didn't have much staff available to speed up the process for checking in forty-three people at the same time. My heart went out to all of them, especially those who weren't feeling well. My eyes scanned the hotel lobby, studying all of their faces. Most of them were truly kind, never complaining, as they stood for such a long time waiting to check into their room.

Randy, Josh, and Matt assisted people to their rooms by carrying their luggage. Emily and I remained in the lobby, chatting with those checking in, and pointing them in the direction of their room. As we said "goodnight" to each person, we also gave a designated time to meet in the lobby of the hotel for breakfast, which was only a few short hours away.

Not many hours later, nearly everyone was in the lobby, grabbing some coffee to help relieve their fatigue from such a short night's sleep. Some looked better rested than others, and I was not one of those people. As I was trying to fall asleep the night before, I was disturbed with worry. I began to question, *what if some people don't receive any healing? Especially those with life threatening illnesses?* I don't know why, but this thought had never really crossed my mind before. I was still preoccupied with this question the morning of the healing service.

From across the lobby, Emily noticed something was wrong and shot me a look as if trying to tell me 'to get it together.' The sinking feeling I was having must have been written all over my face. She came walking straight over to me insisting that I let go of whatever was so evidently bothering me. Emily in no uncertain terms put me in my place, "Mom, please stop it. Whatever it is that is bothering you, simply trust God. He has led us this far and will continue leading us through the remainder of our journey. Just trust!"

I smiled at the incredible amount of wisdom she had for such a young lady. I told her, "You're a hundred percent correct. I'm sorry."

She gave me a quick hug, and thanks to Emily and her insight, I was back to myself in no time, which was perfect timing since we needed to start preparing to leave for the healing service. Soon after, we announced to our group that they should each start heading out towards the bus. Smiles and enthusiasm immediately appeared on everyone's faces as we walked outside together. Emily and I exchanged looks of our own excitement, knowing what a special day this was going to be. Once it looked like we had everyone on the bus, Emily and I did our usual head count and gave the bus driver a big thumb's up afterwards, indicating we had every person accounted for and were ready to go.

As we began the short 15-minute drive to our destination, the retreat center, Emily and I clarified what was on the itinerary for the day. We announced that we would take a break about halfway through the service to have lunch, and then resume until everyone received a prayer. We also appealed to each of them to surrender everything to God and pray for one another throughout the day.

Next, Emily and I discussed the countless prayer requests and photos that we had received and collected from everyone on the trip. We would present all of them to Dr. Nemeh towards the end of the healing service.

Emily held up a rather large envelope to show everyone just how many of them we had accumulated! I explained that I didn't really know how Dr. Nemeh would go about praying over all of them. I imagined he would probably just take the envelope home and pray when he had some time to do so.

Lastly, we shared that after the healing service was completely over, we had a unique opportunity to go out to eat supper with the Nemehs and their volunteers. It was uncommon, given that Dr. Nemeh seldom goes out in public. He normally remains busy at home or in the office, using his time to pray and help others.

When we pulled into the retreat center, the atmosphere immediately felt joyful. It was incredibly uplifting to have the group beaming with excitement as we pulled into the driveway. After the bus came to a stop near the front of the building, Emily and I jumped off quickly to greet Kathy, who welcomed both of us with open arms and an open heart. She gave us both a hug, exclaiming how happy she was to see us again. She talked about how she, her family, and the volunteers had been praying for us ever since we had left Iowa.

Kathy made her way closer to the bus to give a helping hand to those still stepping off. She was all smiles as she happily greeted each person individually. She had such a unique quality in being able to make everyone feel loved and welcomed in a matter of seconds. She made it known that each person was free to roam throughout the building, the chapel, the walking paths outdoors, and the area surrounding the lake. The weather was great, and the place was beautiful! The entire atmosphere provided the perfect backdrop for miracles!

Kathy was quickly encircled by a small gathering of people. This group was made up of their volunteers, which consisted of both family and friends. All at once, I heard a voice that I recognized and remembered from *The Dr. Oz Show* and the *Blind Faith Live* podcasts. It came from a sweet, adorable lady named Kathy Kuack. She had had many miraculous healings of her own and had become a close friend and volunteer for the Nemehs ever since. I was overwhelmed in seeing the large number of volunteers there that day, and the love they had for each other and everyone else was very noticeable. I knew they were there to give back to God and to help others in search of their own miracles.

The volunteers held the front doors open for us as we made our way inside the building. Each one was gracious and friendly. They seemed just as happy to be there as we were. As we walked through the entrance of the retreat center, we proceeded through a narrow hall with restrooms to the left and a staircase to the right that led down to the hall where we would later break for lunch. Continuing forward, the hall branched out into a spacious room that was centered around a fireplace with a floor covered with powder blue colored carpeting. The space was divided in half by three rows of folding chairs set up on each side of the room, exclusively for the healing service.

In the center of the room stood a podium from which Kathy would make introductions and Dr. Nemeh would give a talk about faith. Behind the podium were giant picture windows that extended from the floor to the high vaulted ceiling. The magnificent windows ran the entire length of the room, providing a beautiful view of the grass, trees, lake, and acreage outside.

Kathy introduced Emily and me to some of her children and the volunteers who were there that day. I was surprised by everything, and the healing service hadn't even started! Then Kathy quietly whispered to me that they also had a surprise in store for all of us. I was thrilled! They had already given so much. They just seemed to give so freely and generously beyond any measure. I had never known such loving and charitable people.

Just as Kathy finished speaking with us, we saw Dr. Nemeh come out of a back room. He came over to us, smiling and offering a quick "hello" to Emily and me, and then headed back to a corner in the room near the volunteers. I noticed he stayed more to himself, appearing to be concentrating on the day at hand, and mentally preparing himself for the service of God and others.

Glancing around, I could feel excitement filling the room. This sight reminded me of the first healing service of Dr. Nemeh's that I had attended in 2011. I realized so many sitting there before me in the retreat center were in the exact same boat I had been eight years before. Just like me, they had no idea what to expect. I felt such compassion for everyone patiently waiting for their encounter with Christ that I became exceedingly thankful they each had said "yes" to be there with us.

I was grateful for Emily's comments in the hotel lobby about trust because it reaffirmed my belief in what a powerful experience this would be. I had no doubt that God would bless this beautiful group of people for taking a leap of faith and courage to come on such a long journey in search of His healing. I understood that if anyone didn't receive healing(s) in the way they hoped, they would receive many graces simply from witnessing the power of God in action through Dr. Nemeh's prayers.

Hebrews 11:1 (NRSV)
Now faith is the assurance of things hoped for,
the conviction of things not seen.

twelve.

Who is Closest to Jesus?

THE HEALING SERVICE WAS about to begin. Once everyone was settled in their chairs, Kathy Nemeh began the service by formally introducing herself to our group. She gave us a quick introduction of how she and the doctor had met and become a couple. Kathy concluded this story by saying what a loving and giving person her husband was to everyone.

To explain her husband's character further, she made a reference to a painting that was displayed on an easel right beside her. This was a framed religious print by Tom Dubois titled *Lamb of God*. In this image, Christ is sitting upon a donkey and riding through the street, touching the townspeople's hands as they reach out for Him on Palm Sunday.

Kathy told us how she used to struggle with explaining her husband to people, so she asked Dr. Nemeh, "Who are you? How do you want me to explain who you are to people?"

The doctor left the room and came back with this very same painting of Palm Sunday and asked Kathy, "Who in this picture, Kathy, would *you* want to be?"

She pointed to a few people in the painting, and pointed to one of them in particular, "Well, I would like to be this lady over here. She looks like a pretty cool lady."

Dr. Nemeh asks, "Are you crazy? Who in this picture is closest to Jesus?"

Kathy answers, "Well these two girls holding the flower baskets."

He shook his head and said, "No."

He clarified, "The closest to Jesus in this picture is the donkey. *I am the donkey.* I am the one who patiently carries Jesus to people. No more and no less. I am the donkey."

I had heard this touching association before when I attended the two prior healing services. It is the description Kathy uses to introduce her selfless husband at each service, and I absolutely love it!

It fascinates me at how this man works, thinks, and loves. Most people seem to crave some sort of recognition for what they do. But with Dr. Nemeh's faith, he *knows* God sees every act of love that he does, and that is more than enough for him. He graciously carries love, patience, and humility to everyone he meets. I looked up the description of a donkey in the dictionary and it states that a donkey is a quiet and humble animal at the service of all.

As I stared at this image in greater detail, something caught my eye. I noticed more about the beautiful young girl that Kathy had originally thought was the closest to Jesus. In the painting, this girl is holding a basket of lovely flowers and is ever-so-sweetly dusting the path with flower petals in front of the donkey that is carrying our Lord. This precious little girl is sweetly preparing the path with both beauty and love for the donkey to bring Jesus to the people.

To me, this little girl in the painting resembles Kathy's character. She has an innocent and joyful spirit, and she loves her husband and Jesus in such a beautiful way. Kathy also works hand-in-hand with her husband, introduces him to others, and through her caring words, actions, and love, helps to prepare them as the Lord seeks to enter into their minds and hearts.

After Kathy finished introducing the doctor with such beauty and grace, Dr. Nemeh came up to the front to speak to us. He began with a prayer, and then he started discussing faith-related topics. I know Dr. Nemeh is always inspired on what to say at each healing service, so there is no one talk that is the same.

After he finished, he allowed people to ask a few questions. One man asked Dr. Nemeh if he really wanted to serve God, why didn't he become a priest? Dr. Nemeh explained he feels that he reaches more people by not limiting himself to only one religion. He has people attend his services from every faith and background. I respected his response because we are all God's children.

As he was finishing his opening remarks, the surprise that Kathy had mentioned earlier came walking in the front door. It was Ashley Nemeh. Kathy had asked their daughter, Ashley, to come sing for our group before the healing service. She is an incredibly gifted vocal artist, who is best known for singing Christian music. Ashley stepped up to the front of the room, briefly introduced herself, and began singing a humble Catholic prayer, "Ave Maria," a cappella. Ashley's voice was like that of an angel.

I don't think there was a dry eye in the building when the song came to an end. The song of praise for our Blessed Mother uplifted our spirits and prepared our hearts to receive the Holy Spirit. Ashley graciously thanked each of us for listening and then quickly left, as she had to leave for her next event.

As people continued drying their eyes after listening to Ashley's song, Kathy and the volunteers started rearranging the chairs in preparation for people to receive their individual prayers. They placed ten chairs in front of the room, each facing the giant picture windows overlooking the peaceful view of the large oak trees, walking paths, and beautiful lake.

The volunteers began requesting families with young children and anyone who had mobility concerns to come forward to receive their prayers first. It was a nice gesture, presenting the family or individual with the option to choose how they wished to spend the remainder of their time at the healing service. After their prayer, parents could take a child outside, around the lake, or a person might opt to move to a more comfortable location.

When Dr. Nemeh approached each person, most often he would ask them to stand and share privately with him what he could do for them. As he was praying over each person, it was as if God reached down and created a bubble of silence over that particular person and the doctor. I noticed how this supernatural bubble was created each and every time. What was heard was only what God allowed someone to hear. My family and I were sitting on the right side of the room in the very front row.

Each one of us only heard bits and pieces of each conversation and sometimes, nothing at all, even though we could see the doctor and the person having a discussion. I was always astounded how I never heard anyone's personal information, even if they were willing to share with me later. God wondrously protected each person's privacy.

As Dr. Nemeh began to pray over each person, his hands appeared to be magnetically drawn to where they should go. He wasn't being directed by any person – he was being governed by the Holy Spirit. Many times, someone would try to direct the doctor to the part of their body needing a prayer, only to find he had beaten them to it with his hands already in that exact same spot. This played out over and over throughout the day. It was astonishing!

He would pray with some people for a few short moments and others for longer periods. I have heard him explain in the past that the Holy Spirit guides him, and he knows and even feels when it is time to move on to the next person. Now and then, a person would sit back down in their chair in the midst of their prayer, as being led by the Spirit to do so. Occasionally, a person would fall back into the hands of a loving volunteer quicker than anticipated. The volunteers stood behind each person as Dr. Nemeh was praying, waiting patiently for anyone who was overcome by the Holy Spirit. When this did occur, they would readily assist in guiding them to rest in the chair behind them. Each person's experience was so different. Some people lingered in the Spirit after the doctor had already moved down the line to other people, while others rested in the Spirit for a matter of seconds.

When Dr. Nemeh approached each person, he was quiet, loving, dignified, and a gentleman in every way. When gazing upon someone "falling in the Spirit," at first glance, it can appear that the person has fainted; however, they never really lose consciousness. It is, in my mind, almost the complete opposite because it actually gives the person a more heightened sense of awareness. The worries of the mind and the energy of the body surrender to greater gifts, to those of spiritual peace and physical healing.

Midway through the service, we took a break and went downstairs for lunch. Kathy brought a wonderful spread of food for the group including many types of sandwiches, salads, fresh fruits, and various breads. Everything was wonderful and tasted delicious.

During lunch, Emily and I talked with several volunteers and learned about their connections with the Nemehs and why they wanted to volunteer. Each person explained their incredible testimony and personal healing. They all had such love and gratitude in their hearts that they wanted to give back to God by serving others and helping the Nemeh family in their mission. It was so evident that each one of the volunteer's lives had been transformed by God because they shined the light of Christ to everyone they met.

Following lunch, we headed back upstairs to continue with the healing service. As we started up again, people who had been previously prayed over, took on a different role by praying for the others. I watched as some people silently whispered prayers from their lips, while others extended their hands in the direction of the doctor and person he was praying over. We were all joined together in silent prayer. It moved my heart at the sight of people performing such acts of love for one another, especially considering that not only had they once been strangers to Emily and me, but they had also been strangers to each other as well.

Dr. Nemeh patiently took his time speaking and praying with each person. It was amazing to watch him pray with person after person without taking a single break. He always remained focused on the person in front of him. He would lovingly stoop down, bend over, and at times, cradle a person gently in his arms while he prayed, which reminded me of the compassion of Jesus. As I admired Dr. Nemeh's love for others and observed people receiving healings, I realized we were experiencing a small piece of Heaven on earth, just like we had in his office in January.

I was also blessed to witness Dr. Nemeh pray over my husband and three of my children. My two sons had never been prayed over before, but they both had an open mind when they were called up for a prayer. When I watched Randy and my sons receive a prayer, I could tell they each had some tangible encounter with God.

When the doctor reached my daughter for her prayer, she was sitting right next to me, so I was able to hear some of what was said between the two of them. As Dr. Nemeh approached Emily, he had her stand up and inquired how she had been feeling recently, and she answered, "Good."

Dr. Nemeh gave her a sweet smile, replying, "Good."

He began praying without asking what she needed. Within seconds of the prayer, she fell in the Holy Spirit, while a volunteer helped her to keep standing for a bit. Dr. Nemeh kindly asked the volunteer to let her be. Then the doctor himself gently lowered her down into the chair behind her. I could hear him whispering his soft prayers to God.

After Dr. Nemeh finished praying over each person, Kathy asked our group to participate in a Skype session with the doctor and herself, to assist in offering a group prayer for a young teenage girl. This young girl was not someone from our group, but Kathy explained that this girl's mother had desperately reached out to them, requesting urgent prayers for her daughter. All we knew was she had stage IV cancer and was currently being hospitalized. The mother was aware that our whole group would be offering our thoughts, prayers, and love.

During the session, we all bowed our heads, and prayed fervently for this little angel. It was heartbreaking to see this young girl suffering, but it was a beautiful moment to have all of us linked as one through prayer and love.

Following this blessed opportunity, I had Emily present the large-sized envelope that carried hundreds of photos and petitions to Dr. Nemeh. We explained that most of the photos came from the people on our trip, but some had also been given to us by people who were unable to be with us. We had photos of relatives, friends, clergy, politicians, and world leaders, as well as written prayer intentions in our envelope. It was really amazing to think about the multitude of people who would be receiving a prayer, considering the hundreds of people represented in the envelope. Although the majority of these people receiving a prayer might not have known Dr. Nemeh would be praying for them, we knew there were no limits to God's healing touch.

I had originally thought Dr. Nemeh would take the envelope home and pray over them as he saw fit. I wasn't sure how he and Kathy normally prayed over photos and intentions at other healing services. They mentioned that they would be happy to pray for the photos we brought, and then they asked Emily to step up to the front of the room with the big envelope. We all watched, not sure what Dr. Nemeh and Kathy had in mind.

The doctor asked Emily, "Are all of these your photos?"

Emily answered, "No, not all of them."

Dr. Nemeh then asked, "Do you know all of them?"

Emily chuckled and chirped, "No, but I have seen all the photos, and I do know *some* of them."

Dr. Nemeh clarified, "Ah, but you have the intention on your heart?"

"Yes," answered Emily with a pleasant grin on her face, still uncertain what was going to happen next.

He replied, "Okay," while responding to her smile with a sweet one of his own.

Dr. Nemeh was sitting down on a chair facing all of us. He summoned Emily up closer, to stand facing him. Then the doctor invited Emily to place the envelope out in front of him by holding out her arms.

Kathy Nemeh stood behind Emily ready to catch her if she fell in Spirit. The doctor extended his right arm and began praying. As he was doing so, Kathy, who was still standing behind Emily, also began praying. Nearly three seconds later, Emily began to fall back into Kathy's arms. I heard Kathy say to Emily, "I got you honey."

Kathy laid Emily down slowly and gently, like a feather, onto the soft blue carpeting.

Emily was on the floor, clutching the envelope of photos inches above her body. Emily had tears streaming down her face, and by now, so did almost everyone in the room. After a few moments, Emily's breathing increased and so did her tears. The doctor looked over at me and motioned for me to go to her. While she lay there resting with the Spirit of God flowing through the photos, no one spoke. The entire room was transfixed on this supernatural event taking place.

Kathy Nemeh broke the silence saying, "Look at how peaceful she is; she is like an angel."

Emily's eyes opened slowly, and she cautiously began to stand up. There were lots of gasps and sighs heard throughout the room after watching this beautiful scene.

Emily confided in me how she could unmistakably feel the love God had for everyone in those photos – causing her to weep. She wept not out of sorrow, but from the immensity of love that God held for each person. It touched her soul in a very real and personal way.

As I finished talking with her, we acknowledged our service had come to the end. Dr. Nemeh and Kathy stayed to speak with those who had questions for them or wanted to chat, while the rest of the group loaded on the bus. I looked over at both of them and marveled at how they were always giving to others, knowing they would be joining us for supper shortly.

During supper, our family was beyond blessed to sit near Dr. and Kathy Nemeh, their son, Wadi, and a husband and wife duo who had been volunteers from the day's service. While we talked and got to know each other more, I couldn't help but notice the remarkable resemblance between Wadi and his father. Wadi is a handsome and distinguished young man and is quite humorous as well. He had us laughing most of the way through our meal. We were captivated by listening to him and the doctor talk about working on innovations together that combined faith with science. It was obvious that Wadi not only had his father's looks, but also his superior intelligence. I sensed the deep admiration he held for both of his parents as he spoke about their daily lives.

We couldn't have had better role models sitting in front of us. The loving way they each served God and others in their lives was inspiring and brought me back to Dr. Nemeh's reference to the donkey. Dr. Nemeh's mission to bring Jesus to people should certainly serve as an example for us to follow and ask ourselves the question, "How can each of us contribute to the Kingdom of God?" Each of us has something to give.

Our conversation throughout dinner was focused on faith-related topics and the miracles God had graciously bestowed on others. When supper ended, it was time to say our goodbyes to our sweet friends, Dr. Nemeh, Kathy, Wadi, and the volunteers, Kris and Ken. Even though Emily and I were saddened to leave, we knew we would always hold Dr. Nemeh and Kathy, their children, and the volunteers deep within our hearts. The way they all truly live and practice their faith made a lasting impression on us and encouraged us to become more loving, faithful servants of God.

1 Corinthians 16:14 (NRSV)

Let all that you do be done in love.

thirteen.

What's Your Story?

THE BUS ARRIVED IN front of the hotel for our last night's stay.
After our eventful day, Emily and I made an announcement to the
group that whoever wanted to meet with us in the lobby to share their
experiences and thoughts from the healing service was encouraged to do
so. We explained that we understood if people would not be able to
socialize because we had had a long, emotional day and very little sleep
the night before. We suggested that anyone interested could go to their
room, freshen up, and have some down time before meeting us in the
lobby.

My family and I made sure everyone came off the bus with all their
necessary belongings for the night. Then we went to our hotel room to
change and talk privately as a family before returning to the lobby. I
overheard Randy, Josh, and Matt discuss what each one of them had felt

during their individual prayers. Each one of them recounted detecting intense heat during the prayer, but in different areas of their bodies. My husband described having heat go throughout his entire body while my sons noticed heat in their knees and around their heart. Enthusiastically, they compared their experiences with one another. It was heartwarming for me to hear them connect over spiritual events. I hated to interrupt them, but we needed to get back to the lobby as we had promised.

We were pleasantly surprised when we arrived in the lobby to see many from our group already gathered and talking with one another. At one point, half the group was with us. It was uplifting to see people who had once been strangers become a community and share their experiences with each other.

As the number of people coming into the lobby continued to grow, the group seemed to divide itself into two different sections. Randy, Josh, and Matt all drifted toward the men in the group, while Emily and I stayed with the women. I looked over at my husband and two sons and was pleased to see another opportunity had presented itself for them to bond over their own spiritual encounters.

The men and women splitting into separate groups seemed to help people be more open in sharing their stories. One woman named Patty felt more comfortable sharing her background with other women as she explained that she had three sisters who had suffered with cancer, one of them being triple negative breast cancer, which is especially deadly. Since Patty had a higher risk for cancer, she had more scans than what is normally routine. She said that during a recent checkup, her doctor found a lump, and she had a biopsy scheduled just one week away. She decided to attend this healing service first, hoping that if she had breast cancer, the prayers could potentially help save her life.

She confided in us that when Dr. Nemeh asked what she needed from him, she didn't mention the lump, the breast cancer scare, family history, or the scheduled biopsy. Patty said she trusted that if she had cancer and God desired to heal her, it would happen no matter what she said or didn't say. So she only told Dr. Nemeh about past wounds that she felt were obstacles to living and loving the way God desired. She reiterated to the group of women around her that she had revealed nothing concerning her current condition to Dr. Nemeh, saying, "I never mentioned a word about *any* of it. *Nothing!*"

She told us as soon as Dr. Nemeh began to pray, his hand went directly to the exact spot, like a magnet, and suspended in the air right over the lump itself. She was astounded that the Holy Spirit guided him so perfectly! She explained that was when the intense heat came. It started radiating extreme warmth right there in the same location and it was a deep, piercing heat. It lasted for nearly a minute. She wasn't sure if the lump was being healed, or perhaps the Holy Spirit was pouring love into her heart. Either way it was beautiful! I couldn't help but notice when she was speaking about this, she looked incredibly full of hope. She said she was now looking forward to going in for her biopsy, not for the test so much, but definitely for the results.

We also had two more family members with us on our trip besides my husband and three kids. A few days before leaving for Ohio, Randy had been able to talk his parents into coming on the trip with us. They each had several of their own health concerns, so we were all grateful that they were willing to accept Randy's invitation.

Six years ago, my mother-in-law, Kathy, had had a severe stroke. She had done an amazing job with her recovery. However, she experienced nerve damage on the left side of her body. Since she is left-handed, this presented her with numerous trials along the way. During the healing service, Dr. Nemeh approached her and asked her to remain seated in her chair. As he was ready to begin praying, her eyes closed shut. Since I have seen this happen in others and even felt it in myself, I recognized she was already in the Spirit, but what I didn't know was something incredible was about to happen in the midst of her prayer.

Kathy was about to partake in a captivating and coordinated rhythm with Dr. Nemeh. The doctor took one of his hands and positioned it directly above Kathy's left hand. He had his hand perfectly aligned over hers, but left it suspended in the air. Dr. Nemeh slowly began to elevate his hand, going in a straight line from Kathy's, and moving it straight up a few inches. As he did so, Kathy's hand conformed with his, following along in the same speed and at the same distance. Their hands seemed connected somehow, as Kathy's hand followed and tracked each movement of the doctor's hand.

He would gently move his hand in short, up-and-down movements, and then side to side. My mother-in-law's hand accompanied the doctor's in the same synchronized patterns of movement. Their hands were completely in sync with one another. Throughout this experience, Kathy's eyes remained closed. The doctor never spoke a word, nor did he ever touch her hand.

Emily and I could hardly blink as we watched this beautiful, graceful performance involving the Holy Spirit and their hands. Kathy's eyes opened as she came out of the Spirit. She immediately grabbed her left hand with her right hand, forcing it to lay down on her lap since it was still balanced in the air. I don't think she knew what had just happened. Emily and I were both shedding tears as we marveled at the wonder of seeing God work through Dr. Nemeh.

My father-in-law Gary had his own reasons for coming to the service. He suffered with painful arthritis in his back and knees. When it was Gary's turn to be prayed over, the doctor had him stand up. Dr. Nemeh began his prayers over my father-in-law's back. Within minutes, Gary began to stand taller and taller. He was standing straighter and taller than I had ever seen him stand. While this was going on, there were some cracking noises near his ribs. I was aware that he had recently had a terrible fall and broken several ribs. As they were seemingly snapping back into place, Dr. Nemeh never touched him. It reminded me of the healing service I had attended in January where the lady's back seemed to crack and sound like popcorn. This wasn't that extreme, but I heard similar sounds. That night, Gary shared with us that his back felt the best it had in years.

The last story from our group came from a teenage girl who was there with her family. This girl had really been struggling with a deep depression, but no one, not even the girl herself, knew or could explain why she felt the way she did. She came from a close-knit and very loving family with an incredible deep sense of faith. As her mental state had worsened, the family was at a complete loss about what they could do to help her. They were trying every possible solution to get her the help she needed. This trip offered a fresh approach to the exhaustive medical procedures and tests they had previously tried.

In the lobby of the hotel, the young girl's mom shared that after the prayer service, Dr. Nemeh went out to search for them. He had something he wanted to tell them about their daughter's condition. After he found them, he explained that their daughter was experiencing a neck injury causing a lack of blood supply to her brain. He also recommended specific medical professionals that specialize in this area, who he believed would help her over time.

Even though the parents of this young girl knew their child's condition still needed treatment, they were hopeful because they finally understood the root cause of the problem and how to find the proper help for their daughter. They were also extremely grateful to God for the healing service opportunity and for Dr. Nemeh's medical and spiritual insight. Since this family shared their story, I later reached out and heard that they found a promising, helpful medical program that was originally suggested by Dr. Nemeh.

I am not sure what time it was when we all decided to call it a night, but I am confident that many people's lives were touched that day and will never be the same. During the many hours we spent together that night, I could feel God's presence among us and the incredible joy within everyone's hearts. Each person had their own story and testimony to share, which I believe strengthened our faith and unity in Christ.

John 19:35 (NRSV)

He who saw this has testified so that you also may believe.

His testimony is true, and He knows that he tells the truth.

fourteen.

God's Not "Done"

WE ARRIVED BACK IN Iowa safely late that Sunday evening. Thankfully, the sun was still out, permitting people to safely drive home from our final bus stop. As we said our goodbyes and exchanged promises to stay in touch with one another, we asked the group to please update us with any healings in the days and weeks ahead.

The following day was Memorial Day. I was hoping the people who had come with us would be able to have the day off and rest after our weekend travels. As exhausted as Emily and I were, I thought we would catch up on sleep, but that was far from the truth. I was completely restless with the idea that we needed to schedule another bus trip. I had no doubt God was calling us to do another one, but what I did agonize over was how to ask Kathy for another grand favor, especially after everything they had given us this past weekend. I managed to push through my insecurities, wanting to do as God willed, and found the courage to email her again.

Email to Kathy Nemeh on May 27, 2019

Dearest Kathy,

Hi there my sweet friend! I sure will never be able to thank you and your family and all the volunteers enough for what you did for us this past weekend (as well as the weeks leading up to the healing service). It was incredibly beautiful and so personal. Having Ashley sing was such a surprise and I was speechless because of it! The retreat center was incredibly charming, however I never even made it outside. I had been praying for these new family/friends for so long (even before we met them). It was incredibly moving to see them being prayed over that I could hardly move with the healing service in progress.

I could write you about one hundred different thank you's for all that you did. It was the best day!!! At supper time, I could hardly believe we were sitting at a restaurant with you guys. One reason is Dr. Nemeh hardly goes anywhere, I know, and he made time to come there... that was so meaningful in itself. But to be with you, Dr. Nemeh, and your son, and well, all of it...I had a hard time concentrating on what to order, let alone eating my meal. I wished we could've sat with you all for hours longer. I loved it all so much! To explain how I feel about you guys is to say that you all feel like family to me; Family that I haven't seen for many, many years and we had just been reunited again. I don't know how else to put it into words. After we left the restaurant, it was extremely hard to contain the tears of sadness of leaving you guys again.

I have had dreams and even visions of doing this type of bus trip again, and wanted to talk about it with you, one on one, when we there on Saturday, but couldn't find the right moment of discussing it. I felt like you already knew somehow...did you? ...You mentioned you could see us doing a similar event like this again, which probably was the perfect time, but I hesitated to speak at that moment.

Emily and I were visiting about it and wondered if it was possible to maybe do it again before Emily goes back to school in late August? It should be easier this time around I would think for many reasons.

Many people on the trip asked about the possibility of you guys traveling out to Iowa, but it is so evident to us how busy you all are and that you are needed there. We also realize that reaching the most possible people is probably highest priority, especially considering the times we live in. I would love for you to come out our way, but only when, and if, you felt the timing was right. I guess only time...and God... will tell.

Please let me know what you think. In the meantime, we will pray for you, Dr. Nemeh, and your gorgeous and loving family.

Much love and gratitude to you and your family!
Christy & Emily

Much to my astonishment, Kathy emailed back the same day. Here is her lovely response:

Dear Christy,

I know, we didn't have much time to talk, it was a busy, beautiful day. I'm so happy that you were happy with the whole day. The volunteers loved being there with all of you. They all texted to be sure you arrived safely. I sent a group text upon your arrival home.

The volunteers all love spending time with the Doc and those in attendance. We are so blessed by all of them.

I would love to host another "private" healing service, only before Emily goes back to school. She is truly an angel. I just love that girl of yours! I will call the retreat center tomorrow in hopes of something will be available on a Saturday again.

You and Emily start praying for a date!! Would July work?

I loved every minute with all of you. You are truly a very gifted and special lady! Your faith and love for others, truly made this happen.

You are all in my prayers!

Love, blessings, and prayers,
Your friend and sister in Jesus and Mary,
Kathy

After receiving this amazing email, Emily and I together wrote our response back to Kathy, while trying to contain our excitement. The following message was our response . . . only thirty minutes later:

Hi Kathy,

We would so love to have another healing service trip in August or July. Please let me know what you find out and we will go from there. Emily and I are already praying for the next trip as well as the date and the people.

You are a very amazing woman! We had many beautiful comments about you from the people on the trip! They all loved you so much! They could feel your love and care for others. You two make a perfect team!

One factor I forgot to mention, we heard over and over from so many in the group about how much they loved Dr. Nemeh's talk. They talked about it all the way home on the bus ride.

I thought for sure I would sleep in this morning after the trip, but the good Lord woke me up with a song in my heart and an excitement about the possibility of doing this all over again! I was way too excited to sleep! That's been my life for the last month or so! I love it!!!

Thank you so very much!
Blessings,
Christy & Emily

First thing the next morning, we had a date, a bus, and the same Catholic retreat center all set for this second bus trip. It was amazing how fast things moved when we followed where God was leading us. This time our date landed on the Fourth of July weekend. The healing service was scheduled for Saturday, July 6. We had five weeks to publicize the event and find whomever God had chosen to go on this new trip for more healings and miracles. The Nemehs, Emily, and I all started praying immediately for the people God destined to be on this next trip.

At the beginning of this journey of taking others to see Dr. Nemeh for healing, I thought that one trip was it, and then we would be "done." I never thought any further than that, and I would have never guessed that God would call us to host another trip, especially so soon. For Emily and me, Jesus Himself was our motivation and the purpose behind the first Blessed Reason Trip, and He would continue to be the center of our everything. We had faith that He would guide us towards the people He would be calling on this second trip and that they would be truly transformed by the Holy Spirit.

1 John 5:14-15 (NRSV)

And this is the boldness we have in Him, that if we ask anything according to His will, He hears us. And if we know that He hears us in whatever we ask, we know that we have obtained the requests made of Him.

fifteen.

Divine Providence

IN THE BEGINNING STAGES of planning for the second Blessed Reason Trip, I believed this time around would be simpler and require less effort. In some ways, this was the case, because we didn't have to start from scratch, and I had gained some experience making large group reservations. We knew the only way forward was to stay under God's guidance and to pray our way through each and every step.

During the previous trip, the most challenging part was searching for the people God intended to come with us. However, I was under the impression that this trip would be less demanding on our end. After what people had experienced at the first healing service, I expected there would be many people rushing to sign up on their own and we would have a bus full in no time. I was sorely mistaken, and my expectations were unrealistic for many reasons.

To be included in God's plans meant I had responsibilities and tasks to perform. In order to have opportunities to learn and grow spiritually meant I had to get out and make an effort, instead of sitting around waiting for things to magically work out. God was waiting on me to step forward in faith again, trusting that this was His plan and all things would be for His glory, not mine.

Emily and I continued attending daily Mass, and many times were directed on who to talk to and when. Strangely, I had a sense that God desired a few of the same people who went with us the first time to come again on the second trip. This feeling persisted, and the Holy Spirit began to reveal some of these individuals' names not just to me, but also to Emily. We knew we had to act and say something. The first person we approached was a man named Butch.

Butch and his wife Mary Lou had joined us on the first trip to Ohio. They are the sweetest and most thoughtful couple. When we left for Ohio back in May, Mary Lou and Butch brought a crucifix to place at the front of the bus to offer divine protection for the safety of our travels to and from Ohio.

We learned that Butch was given his name mostly due to his trade, as he is a retired barber and is still known to do a few haircuts here and there inside their home for close friends and family. One day, after Mass, I knew I absolutely had to tell him that they should be coming with us on the second trip. When I told Butch, his response was, "Why would I ever want to go again? Been there, done that."

He hadn't received the healing he was searching for in the first go-round, but he did tell us that he had received an incredible sense of peace in the midst of his prayer. He showed his appreciation for the invitation by giving me a hug goodbye. As he walked out the church doors, I turned to his wife Mary Lou and discovered she was in tears. She told me that she felt they were both supposed to go again and that she would for sure like to join us, but they would have to see how events played out over the next few weeks. We all agreed that we would continue praying for God's will and for the Holy Spirit to guide them both on what they should do.

After several days had passed by, Butch approached me, admitting that he was now praying about coming on the trip because there was a certain stirring in his soul about it. He indicated he was going to check on what their kids had planned for the Fourth of July weekend. Their kids were grown and always made plans that included him and his wife. He explained if, for some reason, their kids hadn't made any plans with them this year, this would be his sign from God that they should come.

The week of the trip, both Butch and Mary Lou approached us saying that they were coming on the second bus trip after all. Their children were all busy and had never made any plans with them. Butch affirmed this was the first time that had ever happened. I recognized it as Divine Providence because God was accomplishing His will through Butch's family. He had most definitely been given his sign and didn't need me or anyone else to tell him that God wanted him to go on this second trip with us. He got the message loud and clear. Emily and I both *knew* there was a special healing waiting for Butch in Ohio.

Another person that we knew should come again was a man named Tom Henneberry, who had come by himself on the first trip. We never approached him, but we were aware that God was calling him back to Ohio for a second time. A few days later, after daily Mass, Tom approached us to ask a few questions about our future trip. He indicated that he wanted to come again, and this time, bring his wife. Tom explained that on the first trip, he thought he had a smaller miracle happen, but it was short-lived, and he wanted to go again. It was only a few days later when he and his wife Linda officially signed up. I was thankful Tom heard God's calling, invited his wife, and decided to come again.

One night before our first trip, Emily had an experience where God specifically called a person by name. The incident happened when Emily was upstairs getting ready for bed, brushing her teeth. All at once, she was given a specific name, precisely as it had happened to me in the past.

She had never heard this name before and questioned who it was. She ran downstairs and asked me, "Mom, I have a weird question, but do you know what a 'Flickinger' is?"

I laughed at the way she phrased her question, and answered, "Yeah, I do actually. That is the last name of a lady that goes to the church where I used to work. Why?"

Emily reported as certain as could be, "The name Flickinger was just given to me and now I know she is supposed to go on our trip."

I sat in silence staring at Emily for a moment. I was completely stunned at what she had said although I shouldn't have been surprised considering how God had been guiding us. A week before the first bus trip, Emily and I had reached out to this lady, Nancy Flickinger, inviting her to go on the trip, but she was unable to join us due to a severe head cold. She was disappointed she was unable to go, but once she heard about this second trip, she signed up immediately.

After she signed up, we decided to explain to her the whole story about why we knew she was to come with us and how her name had been revealed to Emily. She didn't know what to say. I wondered if she honestly believed what we told her, but it didn't matter. We knew the truth and the fact that God was calling her to join us for a blessed reason.

As the days approached for our second bus trip, we had a few more people reach out to us, asking if they could go in place of a loved one. They hoped to receive a prayer on behalf of another person in need. I felt this was an incredible act of love and true faith in God's healing touch. I asserted that this was a very honorable intention and definitely accepted at the healing service.

We knew by now that there were no exceptions, such as going on the bus to intercede for someone else, as God is the one answering people's prayers and doing the healing. All is possible with God, especially if we have the right intentions and love in our hearts. We had at least three people that we knew of sign up on the second trip for this sole purpose, to take the place of a beloved family member or friend. What a beautiful and selfless gift to give someone!

With only a week before our departure date, we decided to reach out to everyone on our mailing list via email. We shared that during the first healing service, many miracles took place due to Dr. Nemeh's prayer over the envelope with photos and petitions. We also wanted them to know that we would be taking all of the original photos again for another prayer and asked if they had any additional photos that they would like us to bring this time.

It didn't take long before photos started coming to us through various letters in the mail, texts, and emails. We had people stopping us after Mass or other random places handing us photos of their family and friends. It was very moving to witness the love and care people had for others by offering photos and intentions of others unable or unwilling to go in order to receive an intercessory prayer from Dr. Nemeh and our group. Our intentions are so powerful when we turn to God in prayer. Through Him, we are all connected by Love.

1 John 4:16 (NRSV)
So we have known and believe the love that God has for us.
God is love, and those who abide in love abide in God,
and God abides in them.

sixteen.

Love Runs Deep in Ohio

THROUGHOUT THE FINAL WEEK before our second trip, our numbers continued to climb. The day we left for Ohio, we had an official count of forty-four people. We felt this was a good amount, considering we just come back from our first trip and hadn't planned this next trip too far in advance. As we began our second Blessed Reason Trip to Ohio, everyone had high spirits and a positive attitude.

I soon discovered the types of healing people were seeking on this journey were as diverse as the people on the bus. We had someone who had a disability and was confined to a wheelchair; another who had recently had surgery that left her without the ability to speak; someone who suffered with severe, unrelenting pain; a young child troubled with seizures; several people with cancer; as well as many others coping with emotional turmoil. There was also a wide range in ages, from six to eighty-six years old.

Before we arrived in Ohio, Butch asked if he could make an announcement to everyone. I was more than happy to give him the microphone to do so, although I was curious about what he was going to say. He began by introducing himself to everyone and admitted that this was his second trip to visit Dr. Nemeh because he hadn't received the healing he was looking for the first time out.

He went on to explain how he was in the midst of reading the book about Dr. Nemeh, *Miracles Every Day*, which I had loaned out to anyone interested. He hadn't read the book before, but now he thought he should. He told us when he was about halfway into the book, he figured out what he may have done "wrong" during the first visit. He wanted to share this idea with the group, to hopefully help others receive the healing they were seeking.

Butch said that in the book, *Miracles Every Day*, Dr. Nemeh specifically says, "Many people come to me for a healing for personal reasons and it will not happen."

Butch shared how during the first healing service he wanted a healing, but only for selfish reasons. He had experienced constant back pain for several years and was on pain medication, but he wanted to be healed so that he could play golf better and have fewer aches and pains. It was all about him rather than God. He continued by saying, "Please, please do not make your healing personal. Make it about God. I don't know *how* you can do this, not make it personal, except to pray about it."

Then Butch returned the microphone to me and sat down. I noticed that Butch's insight seemed to make a rather large impact on the whole group. Everyone was silent and appeared to be contemplating his powerful words and how they could be applied to themselves.

The healing service began the next morning with Kathy Nemeh introducing herself, the volunteers, and then her husband. Dr. Nemeh said a prayer before he spoke and then went right into talking to us about the urgency of the era we are living in right now. He informed us, "We are very blessed to be living in these times."

After he finished speaking, they began the prayer service. First, Dr. Nemeh proceeded by stepping to the side to pray over a relative of two of the volunteers. He was an older gentleman who was confined to a wheelchair. When Dr. Nemeh finished praying over him, he moved to the front of the room to begin praying over the people from our group, who were sitting quietly and respectfully waiting for their individual prayer.

A few moments after Dr. Nemeh had moved on to those sitting in the front of the room, we heard someone start speaking to the crowd. It was the same man in the wheelchair that Dr. Nemeh had first prayed over. His voice was loud enough that we could all hear him. I was not at all prepared for what he was about to say. He stated, "I am not sure if you all knew this or not, but Dr. Nemeh's father passed away last night. The doctor is such a giving person that he has decided to spend the day with all of you, instead of being with his family and grieving with them."

There were a few immediate audible gasps throughout the room. Many were in shock and exchanged looks of sadness about the loss of Dr. Nemeh's father.

He continued speaking, "I probably wasn't supposed to tell you this, but I wanted you to all know what kind of a person you are dealing with. These are the most generous and loving people I have ever known."

Nearly all of us in that room began to cry. I think many of us were deeply moved as we realized the true, selfless love this man, Dr. Nemeh, carries for people. I looked over at the doctor and noticed how he remained focused on what he was doing. He continued praying with the particular individual that was in front of him, even while the man was still speaking and people were crying. He never missed a second of staying in constant prayer and completely anchored in the Holy Spirit.

I, on the other hand, was not very steady. Due to my strong emotions, I was unable to remain seated and needed a moment to regain my composure. I quickly moved out of my chair, making my way out of sight, while trying with all my might to contain my own sadness. Quickly, I became aware that it wasn't only the sadness that was affecting me; it was the doubts that had been assaulting me for weeks about this trip.

The fears that I once had in the past seemed to resurface in an instant. I began second guessing myself that maybe we shouldn't have had another bus trip. I thought I had done pretty well getting rid of these uncertainties, but now it was apparent that they still lingered deep inside me. The doubts, fears, and uncertainties that I had worried about throughout this entire process were crushing.

I looked for a place to hide so I could attempt to pull myself back together. I was responsible for this special group of people and knew I needed to act as such. I walked out through the first set of doors and tucked myself into a breezeway between the next set of entrance doors to the building. There were a few chairs within this entry space, and I sat down in one, ashamed of how I was letting this happen to me.

One of the volunteers named Jessica, who is often mistaken to be one of Kathy's beautiful daughters because of her comparable beauty and sweet charm, ran after me to console me during my emotional breakdown. She sat beside me, placed her arm around me, and hugged me as I sobbed into my hands for a few moments. Thankfully, she didn't waste any time in encouraging me with loving words of wisdom, showing me that despair was neither needed, nor did it serve any purpose. Jessica spoke to me in a warm, caring way, while adding vital words of caution. She asserted, "Don't you dare. Don't you dare listen to that voice."

I knew right away that somehow she recognized that the reason I was so upset was that I was questioning whether we should even be there at all.

She went on, "I have been around the Nemehs long enough to know that when an event isn't supposed to happen, or someone isn't supposed to be around them . . . it doesn't, and they aren't. If you were not supposed to be here today, believe me, you wouldn't be here. You would have had a flat tire, or the bus would have broken down. Something, somewhere, would have gone wrong, to prevent you from being here today. Believe me, *I know.*"

She continued, "This is how things work around them. You are *meant* to be here! These beautiful people you brought here today are *meant* to be here. This is all for a reason. Don't you listen to those doubts in your head! Ever! Don't ever think like that again. *Everything* works for God's glory with the Nemehs."

Her words were incredibly profound and inspiring and left a long, lasting impression on me. She continued hugging and consoling me, because at that point, even more tears were falling. They were no longer tears of sadness, but tears of gratitude. It was so considerate of Jessica to come after me and share this truth.

Her encouraging words helped me pull myself together. This was yet another lesson for me, one that I will never ever forget, as her words still echo in my heart to this day. Jessica, at that moment, was an absolute godsend.

Jessica and I walked back into the healing service. Kathy Nemeh could see I had been crying, grabbed me by the hand, and brought me with her to the front of the room to make an announcement.

I knew Kathy also sensed the struggles I had been wrestling with inside myself. She kept holding my hand as she spoke to the room emphasizing, "You are all *meant* to be here. We knew the doc's father wasn't doing well, and we knew he was probably going to pass this last day or so. I asked Dr. Nemeh if we should cancel the healing service. His reply was, 'No. It is meant to be.'"

Kathy continued, "We weren't going to say anything until the end of the healing service, so nobody was distracted from this beautiful day. We have decided to dedicate this healing service to his father, Wadi Nemeh, as we know he is here praying with Dr. Nemeh for all of you."

She continued by telling us that her own mother had had a heart attack the night before as well and was in a local hospital as she spoke. Kathy told us she *knew* that she was meant to be here with us as well. She pointed out that her mom was in good hands because there were other family members staying with her at the hospital, while she and Dr. Nemeh spent this incredibly special day with us.

Dr. Nemeh and Kathy are the most loving, giving people. I can't think of anyone who would be so charitable as to sacrifice their time with loved ones in the midst of two family emergencies so that they could offer their love, care, time, and attention to complete strangers.

The Nemeh's mission in life seemed to be fully recognized in that moment. Their lives beautifully represent the way Christ calls each of us to love as He has loved us. I will never forget how generous these two people and their families were to us that day.

During lunch, it was beautiful to see the fondness and friendship Dr. Nemeh and Kathy had for each other. They also spent time with their beloved volunteers, who were also apparently very close and dear friends of theirs.

Kathy stopped by our table for a minute to share how the volunteers were doing their best to keep the doctor in good cheer by sharing funny stories about Dr. Nemeh's father. I looked over, and sure enough, the doctor was smiling and even chuckling.

At that moment, Kathy Kuack (Kathy K.), who had also been at the first healing service, came over to our table and pulled up a chair. After listening to her share stories on the *Blind Faith Live* podcasts about herself, her family, and the Nemehs, I felt like I already knew her. Kathy K. was beyond grateful for her life-saving, life-changing miracles, including being healed of lung cancer. I believe she had had a longer list of autoimmune disorders as well as other diseases and ailments.

Kathy K. shared with everyone at our table some of what she has seen, heard, and experienced while being around the Nemehs for so many years. She revealed miracle story after miracle story.

The stories that seemed to touch me the most were not necessarily about miraculous healings, but about people's faith. Kathy K. told us that often people will call the doctor's office and ask if they can just come sit in the waiting room for a little while to read their Bible or to sit and pray. People have such a strong desire to be near the heavenly events that take place in Dr. Nemeh's office. That was so endearing to me. What immense faith people have! I could only imagine how much this must touch the Nemeh's hearts, let alone God's.

After lunch, we went back upstairs to pick up where we left off with the healing service. A short while later, an extraordinary and instantaneous healing took place in front of the entire group. It happened to a very sweet woman in our group named Bonnie Troe. She had laryngeal cancer and recently had her voice box surgically removed, so she was unable to speak. After Bonnie received her prayer, she went back to her original seat. Within a few minutes of sitting down we could hear her speak with a compromised, softer, and almost hushed voice exclaiming, "I can talk! I can talk! I can talk!"

It was a miracle because Bonnie had no physical way of producing a vocal sound. Yet we could hear her speak each word as she raised her hands in praise and excitement.

Everyone that could hear her and knew what was going on started crying tears of joy. Dr. Nemeh, who was in the middle of praying over someone, heard the commotion, looked up with concern and compassion, and asked what was wrong. Someone explained to him how this woman had been healed and that she had a voice again.

He simply gave a smile at God's blessing and continued on praying with the person in front of him. For him, this was a normal daily occurrence. Multiple times throughout each day he witnesses miracles happening, so it was no surprise to him whatsoever, but he always gives thanks and all glory to God.

Bonnie had been struggling with the anguish of losing her voice in recent months. Not only this, but it had been quite a challenge to learn how to communicate in a different manner since her surgery. Everyone was extremely moved by God restoring her voice, even if it might only be temporary, to uplift her spirits and show her that He was with her.

In recent months, I have heard that her voice comes and goes, but the peace she gained from her prayer with Dr. Nemeh has remained with her ever since. That peace speaks volumes to those who know her and her circumstances. It was a wonderful reminder that there are no limits with God!

At the end of the service, Ashley Nemeh surprised us, as she had on our first trip, by showing up to sing for our group. I could tell how the past few days were weighing on her, with her grandfather's death and her grandmother's hospitalization. After everything their family had been through, she still sang with grace and radiant joy. I was incredibly touched by the amount of sacrificial love this entire family was willing to give to all of us.

Before Ashley began singing, we mentioned to the doctor and Kathy that we had brought more photos with us. Kathy and Dr. Nemeh couldn't believe the amount we had as the envelope was nearly twice the size compared to our first trip. Kathy and the doctor had Emily come up to the front of the room right in the middle of the aisle where the entire group had a clear view. Dr. Nemeh asked Emily to hold the envelope containing twice the number of photos and intentions.

The room became increasingly quiet. It felt as if we were all holding our breath as our hearts offered all the people we had brought with us in this large envelope. Everyone sat silently, eager to see what would happen next as Emily walked up to the two of them. Dr Nemeh instructed Emily how to hold the envelope, while motioning to a volunteer to stand directly behind her in case she fell back in the Spirit.

It was good that they were prepared for Emily's response, since she fell back in a matter of seconds into Dr. Nemeh's prayer and rested in the arms of one of the devoted volunteers. Dr. Nemeh continued praying for a few more moments with his hand outstretched into the air as Emily was gently lowered onto the same blue carpeting as the first healing service.

She rested peacefully, holding the envelope suspended in the air approximately a few inches from her body. The Spirit of God fully encompassed Emily and all of the prayer intentions. She began to tremble and shed tears from the overwhelming love and presence of God surrounding the photos.

While God's grace continued to wash over all the photos, Kathy had Ashley come up and sing "Hail Mary, Gentle Woman." During the song, Dr. Nemeh gestured for me to go to Emily and sit beside her as she continued lying there. I knelt down right beside her and noticed her face was tranquil from this heavenly peace. Then, I heard some individuals nearby whispering and asking if she was okay.

I understood these questions and worries because this phenomenon was new to almost everyone present. After Kathy Nemeh promised that Emily was most definitely okay, several people released a big sigh of relief. It was apparent to me how some of these individuals were beginning to understand that they were witnessing an act of God's love through the Holy Spirit wafting over their loved ones and my daughter. Many of the people were moved to tears by the beauty of everything taking place. It was a most remarkable and heavenly sight.

When Ashley finished singing, Emily was still there lying on the floor right in the middle of the room. She was still resting in the Spirit, her breathing had become deep, and streams of tears continued pouring down her cheeks. Kathy came over to the other side of Emily, knelt down beside her, and prayed, "Come Holy Spirit in the name of Jesus."

This prayer promptly helped Emily to come out of the Spirit. As Emily began to open her eyes, Kathy said in a sweet and loving voice, "There you go, honey."

The whole process was quite emotional for Emily. Later, Emily told us that during the prayer, she could clearly feel the love that our group held in their hearts for the family and friends in the envelope. Once Emily was back up on her feet, she had a few people encircle her and ask if she was in any pain. They specifically questioned if she could feel the pain of the people represented in the photographs. Emily smiled, humbled by their concern, and lovingly responded, "No. It is not painful. Not at all. It's incredible!"

Then some expressed a look of confusion as more questions seemed to emerge. One person wondered why Emily was crying so much, assuming she was probably feeling some sort of discomfort. Emily was inspired to share more of her experience in greater detail with those who were surrounding her. She corrected their misconceptions by announcing, "It simply is just overwhelmingly beautiful!"

Emily took a deep breath, and then said, "The prayers and the feelings I felt were beautiful and powerful. It is more overwhelming because I feel God's love for everyone. You can't help becoming emotional when the Holy Spirit is moving in such a wonderful and exciting way."

People started talking amongst themselves, saying they couldn't wait to hear what miracles resulted from those prayers. They knew they would be powerful based on what they had witnessed.

My mind was brought back to the many obligations that the Nemehs still had ahead of them. They were there with us for close to six hours and they still had to go meet with family from out of town, attend to Kathy's mother, as well as process their own personal grief from the passing of Dr. Nemeh's father. The doctor spoke up just then, and being a man of impeccable faith, informed us that there was no reason to be sad.

His father had been right beside him all day long as he prayed with each person.

When he said this, I was in total awe of his deep, steady faith. Dr. Nemeh seems to only look at events and daily life through his spiritual lens and does not ever doubt. Even so, my heart could not help but ache for him, Kathy, and their entire family.

Similarly, Kathy was just as awe-inspiring to me as her husband! She also had demonstrated great faith in God throughout their entire situation. She was genuinely more concerned about how others were affected by the news than herself. It was as if she expressed motherly love towards everyone, including her family, the volunteers, and our group. Neither Kathy nor Dr. Nemeh appeared sad but seemed quite content to focus their love and attention on others.

Kathy and Dr. Nemeh were clearly happy to be there with us that day and both were unbelievably steady with their emotions and beliefs. They made the entire healing service about every man, woman, and child that was there and never once made it about themselves. They provided such a powerful lesson for all of us. As Christians, we are called to love and care for the needs of others, as our lives are truly all about serving.

As our day came to an end, Dr. Nemeh spoke from his heart, sharing that he loved each one of us. I believe we left that healing service with a new definition of what love is and how we should apply it, living not for ourselves, but for those around us.

After we said our goodbyes at the retreat center, ate supper, and safely arrived at our hotel, Kathy and I briefly corresponded with one another.

Email from Kathy Nemeh on July 6, 2019:

Dear Christy!

What a beautiful day! Truly blessed in every way.

We had a line-up of family and friends in and out of our home all day and into the evening, truly overwhelming in a beautiful way. My father-in-law loved everybody, and everyone loved him.

We are watching the funeral at 7:00 a.m. It's being live-streamed to us.

Please let me know when you depart, so I can start praying.

Thank you and Emily for organizing this very amazing trip!

Love, prayers and blessings,
Kathy

Emily to Kathy Nemeh on July 7, 2019

Good Morning Kathy,

My heart is so very full that I could barely sleep a wink, all I could think of was what you and the doctor gave us yesterday, especially during what was happening in your family! And believe me that's all anyone spoke about last night!

That message speaks volumes of the love you guys carry and bring to others and how much we have to learn from how you and the doctor lead your lives.

One man said it was biblical in nature and reminded him of the story where Jesus asks the man to follow him and the guy first wanted to bury his father. Jesus responded saying let the dead bury the dead, as it was more important to be with Jesus in that moment....so beautiful! Again, my heart is overrunning with gratitude and love for you both and all your volunteers more than I can put into words.

Thank you from the bottom of all of our hearts!

We leave at 10 a.m. but I'll text when we leave and when we get home ...thank you so much for offering to pray for us.

We will all be praying for you guys and I'm so glad they are televising this for you all.... that's so wonderful!!! Emily and I (as well as everyone here) loves you both so very much!

Praying for you both all day and always!
Love to all of you,
Christy & Emily,

Email from Kathy on July 7, 2019

We are watching my dear and amazing father-in-law's funeral "live" from Damascus, Syria. Your beautiful words made me cry. Touch base later.

Love to all of you. Truly a blessed and special day for us and our wonderful volunteers

Kathy

John 13:34-35 (NRSV)

"I give you a new commandment, that you love one another. Just as I have loved you, you also should love one another. By this everyone will know that you are My disciples, if you have love for one another."

seventeen.

The Purpose of a Healing

AFTER A FEW WEEKS had passed since the second Blessed Reason Trip, Emily and I sent out emails to everyone who had gone on the trip and asked them if they were comfortable, to please share with us any healings they may have experienced. Our intention was to forward their stories to the Nemehs, showing them that the seeds of charity and love they planted were now bearing the fruits of love and healing. The Nemeh's amazing ability to stay strong during their time of grief and in the most challenging of circumstances was such an incredible act of love and sacrifice. I wanted to be able to give back to them by sharing the incredible miracle stories that had taken place that day.

Within a few hours of sending this email, people began contacting us. Some of them were quick to notice the transformations in themselves and were ready to proclaim their healing, while others needed more time to reflect on their encounter with God. We also had individuals share some of the miracles that had taken place for the people whose photos had been placed in the large envelope and prayed over. One by one, I began to collect and document all of the healing stories coming through.

A few days later, Butch and Mary Lou Milling caught up to Emily and me after Mass and asked if they could have a word with us before we left the building. The look on their faces gave us a clue that they had some exciting news. Butch was just beaming as he began to speak, "Christy and Emily, I want you to both know something. I am claiming a healing from our last trip to Ohio!"

Emily and I exchanged smiles. We had known there was something special waiting for him, but it was even more exciting to hear him tell us what that was, as we still had no clue. Butch explained that he had suffered from stenosis of the spine and terrible back pain for many years. The agony of this condition was barely tolerable, which had led him to take over twenty-four epidural shots and prescription pain medication every single day for the past two years. Unfortunately, he claimed the medication hardly made a difference.

Since Butch became aware that his healing should serve God instead of himself, he received his miracle. Before making anything public, he wanted to stop all his pain medication indefinitely and test his back. With gratitude and joy, Butch exclaimed that he had been pain-free and free from his prescription pain medication since the healing service in July. To this day, Butch has remained fully healed and has shared his testimony with hundreds of people, including family, friends, and strangers alike.

Shortly after Butch and Mary Lou shared their good news with us, another married couple from our second bus trip, Tom and Linda, came to share their miracle after Mass. Tom joyfully smiled and recounted his story by saying, "Christy, I wanted to tell you that on the first trip I didn't experience a physical healing. At first, I was hoping that I did and tried to stop my medication, but within three days I had a horrible headache, and had to go right back on my prescription for my condition. I did, however, see relationships healing within our family after that trip, and I certainly felt the Holy Spirit working in others."

He continued, "My wife was able to accompany me this time to the second healing service. I hadn't really thought much about my approach to any of this before until Butch took the microphone on the bus on the way to Ohio and shared that quote from Dr. Nemeh in the book. That moment helped me change my thinking. It allowed me to realize that I needed to make this search for a healing to be about my love for God and what more I could do for Him.

"When Dr. Nemeh approached me and started praying over me, I closed my eyes to concentrate on the prayer and I immediately felt an intense heat on my face for several seconds. Since I was standing in front of a huge uncovered window, I thought maybe a cloud had moved that was originally blocking the rays of the sun, but I didn't open my eyes to verify this because I wanted to focus on the prayer.

"I have what is called *cerebral venous sinus thrombosis*. Anyway, since the healing service, I have been completely off all the medication for the blood clot. And the signature headache that I used to have, indicating the presence of a clot, has not returned since."

Later, I looked up the meaning of his diagnosis, and it is a blood clot in the dural venous sinuses in the brain. These sinuses are where blood drains from the brain.

Tom explained to me that the long-term plan from the doctors was originally to keep him on anticoagulants, a type of medication to help him with blood clots, for the rest of his life. At the time of diagnosis, the benefits from taking the prescription far outweighed the risks. This was because the disease that Tom had came with dangerous complications such as stroke, heart disease, and other vascular problems. Even though the prescription helped lower his risks and save his life, it was beginning to affect him, which was ultimately what led him to search for God's healing.

I was astounded by Tom's story as well as his faith. Learning the severity of Tom's condition helped me to understand where he was coming from and the great need he had for healing. I never did inform him that I knew God had huge plans for him on this second trip, but after our conversation, there was no need to, since deep down he already knew.

Based on the timing of Butch's and Tom's miracle stories, it was evident that God wanted to be glorified through these healings when they had taken place. Butch's realization on the bus, based on the quote he had read in the book about Dr. Nemeh, enlightened many to the fact that God doesn't desire to heal us based on our need of good health and selfish desires. Instead, He wants to heal us to teach us the realization that we need Him, and only Him. I believe the main purpose of a healing is the conversion of our hearts.

As I continued to compile the numerous healing stories to share with the Nemehs, several more individuals connected with me from our second bus trip, requesting to meet over coffee, a walk in the park, a quick lunch, or to speak at length over the phone about their experiences. It was uplifting to hear what had happened with each person and to know that helping others learn about Dr. Nemeh was truly making a difference for each of them.

Many people shared with me that they had received a life-changing healing, both emotionally and spiritually. Each person described that they had lived with constant heartache, guilt, anxiety, sadness, grief, and/or anger. They had carried this pain every day, many of them since childhood. It had taken over many aspects within their lives, but most of all, it had affected their relationships, how they conducted themselves, their level of trust for others, and even occasionally, their faith in God.

In the time it took for Dr. Nemeh to pray and the Holy Spirit to bring the healing power of Christ to their souls, their wounds and sorrow were healed. They were left with nothing but a deep sense of peace and well-being, allowing them to forgive and forget, and even love those again who had previously hurt them. These changes weren't necessarily seen on the outside, but there was a transformation that took place within their spirit.

After collecting many healing stories, I sent an email to Kathy about the fruit of our second healing service, which they dedicated to Dr. Nemeh's father. I shared the powerful testimonials to glorify God, and I thanked the Nemehs for their generosity, love, and prayers.

Towards the end of August, Emily returned to college and resumed her studies in Elementary Education, which made me think we were finished with healing services and bus trips for a while. Little did I know, God had bigger and better plans. Nearly two weeks after Emily started her classes, I called her to share the surprising news that God had recently revealed that we were to offer another bus trip. I explained my desire to do as God had requested and wondered if she would like to join me again. Emily agreed and explained she had felt the same way, which prompted me to send another email to Kathy Nemeh.

Email to Kathy on September 2, 2019:

> *Hey there, my Adorable and Sweet Friend,*
>
> *I hope you are enjoying this beautiful weather and are able to relax and perhaps spend time with family?*
>
> *The reason I am writing you is that you tell me to keep following God's prompting and so I am contacting you to check if you all have a date in late October for yet another healing service for us Iowans, and that perhaps the retreat house may again also have an opening?*
>
> *I have had dreams about more bus trips but I kind of dismissed them, because I wondered how this would work with Emily in school and it being so soon after our last one. I finally shared with Emily and she said she was dreaming about bus trips too...and then again this morning it is pressing on my heart along with the words to 'follow and trust'....so here I am.*

Thank you, thank you! Looking forward to hearing your thoughts Kathy!

Many Hugs and Love,
Christy

To my surprise, Kathy responded right away.
Email from Kathy on Monday, September 2, 2019:

Let's plan a bus trip ASAP, before the weather gets bad.

Looks like so far the only weekend free is October 12th! We are booked all the other weekends.

I'll see if Retreat Center is available. Another leap of faith you and Emily are taking. I love your conviction to this mission of yours.

Love you both my dear friends!
Kathy

Within a few hours, we were suddenly and very happily organizing another bus trip to Ohio. This time it would be held in a new location, a Benedictine Monastery in Cleveland.

Even though Emily was a full-time student, she was able to help me prepare for this trip on the weekends. While taking classes and doing homework, she felt college was a great opportunity to share this event with others, so she spoke at social events, including the on-campus priest and congregation, as well as a few individuals she felt God was calling to join us. Due to God's grace, several people heeded the call and signed up.

We had a total of thirty-eight people sign up for this healing service. I knew this upcoming trip in October would help many people to be enlightened, transformed, and live in closer union with Christ. Gradually, I started to understand God's mission for Emily and me, which was to guide others to the Nemehs, not so much for their physical healing, but for the saving grace and truth they find in Christ through their encounter with the Holy Spirit.

Ephesians 1:11-12 (NRSV)
In Christ we have also obtained an inheritance, having been destined
according to the purpose of Him who accomplishes all things
according to His counsel and will, so that we, who were the first to
set our hope on Christ, might live for the praise of His glory.

eighteen.

Need a Sign?

TWO PEOPLE THAT SURPRISED us by signing up on this trip was Butch and Mary Lou. This would be their third trip with us! They did so out of their love for others. Following Butch's amazing healing, they had several of their friends and family members sign up to go on this third trip, and they decided to come and support their loved ones. Both Butch and Mary Lou had been so moved by what took place with Butch and all the other transformations they had witnessed with us in the last two trips, that the two of them had been evangelizing and sharing the good news with everyone they knew. I loved watching how over a period of a few months, this had started to become a type of ministry for them as well.

Many times, Emily and I were given nudges on who was to go on this trip, just as we had in the past. One man, in particular, was someone I would see in church quite often. I had never spoken to him before, nor did I know his name, but on one occasion after Mass when there were many people talking in the grotto area of the church, I noticed him speaking with Butch. Just then, Mary Lou walked up to me and told me that Butch was talking with this same man about our upcoming trip. Immediately, following Mary Lou's words, I had the scent of roses engulf me even though there were no flowers in sight. I turned my eyes to Mary Lou, and with great sincerity said, "This man is *supposed* to be on this trip. I *know* this for an absolute certainty."

Mary Lou, a woman of incredible faith, was able to interpret by the manner I had spoken to her that I had been given a sign from Heaven. I could tell that she knew this just by the look in her eyes and the many tears that were forming. I asked her his name. She informed me that his name was Mike Sevart. I knew deep within me that I was to speak with Mike right then and there. I had no idea what I was even going to say, and as I was trying to think of what that would be, it was like my legs had a mind of their own because I was already walking straight over to him.

As I walked up to Mike and Butch, they had just finished their conversation, and Butch was starting to walk away. I was a nervous wreck at this point, since I still had no idea of how to express what I knew to a stranger, or exactly how I was to invite him to come with us. I began by introducing myself and informing him that I needed to speak with him about something important. I pointed over across the room to Mary Lou, indicating she had told me that her husband, Butch, had just talked to him about our bus trip. Mike nodded in acknowledgement. His eyes desperately searched mine for an understanding of why I needed to speak with him so urgently.

I informed him that I was the organizer of the trip, and today, as I was watching him talk with Butch, something had happened to me. I stopped myself from speaking any further. I could feel myself becoming more nervous with what I was about to say next, but I took a deep breath and pushed through. I looked intently into his eyes for a moment, and then asked, "Do you believe that God gives people signs? Like the smell of roses, for example?"

He looked startled by my question, but his answer was profound.

Mike said, "Absolutely, I do."

After seeing that he believed that God works in mysterious ways, I went on to explain that as soon as Mary Lou had told me that Butch was talking with him about the bus trip, I had an overwhelming smell of roses completely surround me, and I knew *instantly* it had to do with him. I said, "God spoke to my heart right then that you were meant to go on this trip with us."

I gave Mike some more information about our two previous trips. I told him on occasion, there had been a select few individuals, who although were strangers to me, God had directed me to approach them and invite them to sign up for our trip. Each person was called for a different purpose, and the reasons and the way this whole process worked was way beyond my own understanding. I went on explaining, "In this moment, right now, I have come to realize these signs were not meant for me. Instead, they were given to me to share with particular people, to inspire their hearts to trust the way God intended."

I was honest with Mike that I didn't fully understand any of it. I told him that sharing this with him was not at all easy for me, and it was taking me *way* outside my comfort zone.

Mike seemed noticeably touched and he began to lower his guard as I spoke. Following my explanation, he opened up to me about a personal story that involved roses. To him, what I had just revealed was a sign straight from Heaven just for him specifically. At this time, he paused for a minute, and then informed me that he had recently been diagnosed with stage four kidney cancer. I was taken aback by this news as I had no idea. I was beyond thankful he was open and willing to listen to what I had to say. I was honored that he shared his personal story with me, a complete stranger. Mike assured me he would prayerfully consider coming, but he wasn't going to make any promises, and with that he walked away.

After leaving Mass that afternoon, I sat in my car overcome as my emotions ran all over the place regarding my conversation with Mike. I was so moved that he had revealed his serious health diagnosis to me. I was also surprised that I shared the sign I had received from God a few seconds before I approached him, but I knew the Holy Spirit was speaking right through me to him. God knew Mike needed to hear those words. Mike signed up shortly after our conversation.

I came across another person right after my episode with Mike, where I smelled the same scent of roses without any flowers in the room. It all started when I was attending a meeting at a person's house. When I sat next to this certain lady, Gloria, I had that same scent of roses flood my senses. Over and over, it came, five separate times, all occurring within a short two-hour period. The only problem was I was also sitting among twenty other women, so I wasn't one hundred percent sure if it was meant for Gloria, or if it was for someone else. Since I didn't want to tell the wrong person, I chose not to say anything.

A few short days later, I spoke with Gloria alone outside the church, and the same beautiful scent of roses flowed all around me. Even though I was certain it was meant for her all along, I knew the timing wasn't right, so again, I kept quiet. A day later, I was happy when I saw she had signed up on our website to come on the bus trip. *She must have felt God's calling all on her own,* I thought. I was somewhat relieved that I wouldn't have to explain this process again like I had with Mike, as it wasn't very easy for me.

Four days before we were to leave, I attended a Catholic Evangelization Outreach (CEO) meeting one evening in Cedar Rapids. CEO is a Catholic organization that holds monthly events where a speaker is brought in to give a presentation about the extraordinary way that God had stepped into their lives. Following each presentation, they would offer a light dinner during which people could discuss among themselves the powerful witness they had heard.

I felt a last-minute nudge to go to this event. I didn't plan on making any sort of announcement, but I wanted to be there in case someone had questions or needed details about our upcoming trip. I did speak with a handful of people, and as I was about to leave, I noticed a friend of mine struggling with something. Eileen is a sweet, devoted lady, who purchases and provides faith-related books for people who attend these monthly events, all because she feels called to do so out of her love for God and others. Eileen had a table set up with her books, and when people walked by, she handed them out for free.

She struggled trying to get one man's attention as he walked by her on his way out the door. As she attempted to call out to him and hand him the book, his head was bowed down, and it seemed he didn't hear her. I walked over to Eileen and told her that I would be more than happy to go after the man and give the book to him. I caught up with him about halfway down the hall near the entrance of the church.

As I reached him, I explained how he had missed getting a free book. He thanked me, never looking up, and just stared down at the book. As I continued looking at him, I couldn't help but sense a deep sadness in him, and I had the overwhelming feeling to tell him about the healing service. The desire was much more than a simple nudge; it was more like a push.

I pulled out a postcard and flyer from my purse and placed them both on top of the book he was still staring at. I gave him my name, and told him that my daughter and I were putting this bus trip together for a third time for anyone needing healing. I suggested if he was interested, we had plenty of room, and he could look online for all the details about it. I warned him that we were scheduled to leave in a few short days.

I paused, waiting for him to say something. It took nearly a minute before he glanced up from the information I gave him. I saw his eyes were increasingly filling with tears. His far-off stare was slowly beginning to focus in on my eyes. He told me his name was Art, and he had been having many serious medical issues recently. The doctors, unfortunately, had not been able to provide him with any concrete answers as to what was happening with him. They thought perhaps he had an autoimmune disease, but that was only out of pure speculation at the time. He had been all over the place searching for answers, including the Mayo Clinic in Rochester, Minnesota. He uttered an emotional "thank you" and said he thought this trip was just the miracle he had been searching for.

As I left the church that night, I shook my head at God's timing. He never ceased to amaze me with His perfect plan. The day before our departure date, I was overjoyed when I noticed Art had officially signed up online to join our trip.

That same night, Emily and I were busy printing out the last-minute photos that people sent us by email to take with us to be prayed over by Dr. Nemeh. Emily came across a photo of Gloria and her family, whom she had never officially met before. Emily stopped what she was doing, held the photo in her hands, and stared at it for a long minute. She then proceeded to show it to me. Emily said that as she had been gathering the photos, she had picked this one up and smelled a rush of roses. I told her about what had happened to me, and we were both astounded that each of us had had this experience with Gloria. What we didn't realize was that there was a bigger purpose for it yet to come. Gloria had signed up just days earlier and was going to give us her paperwork and payment first thing the very next morning as we prepared to load the bus and head to Ohio.

As Emily and I pulled our vehicle into the church parking lot, with only thirty minutes left to spare before our scheduled departure for Ohio, Gloria approached us looking a bit anxious. She came up rather quickly to our car, and I could see she had a look of panic in her eyes. As Emily and I stepped out of our car, Gloria began speaking fast and asked us if we thought she should *really* be coming. She explained that she had a son at home who had sporting events scheduled during the time she was to be in Ohio with us, and for some reason, all at once, she was stricken with fear that she was making a mistake and now wondered if she wasn't supposed to go.

I knew right then that those experiences with the roses that God had given to both Emily and me were for this exact moment. This is when we were to share with her what had happened. I posed the same questions I had asked Mike previously, "Do you believe in signs from God? Like the smell of roses?"

As quickly as she claimed she did, Emily was the one who picked up from there, telling her what had happened the night before with her photo. Gloria was apparently still in panic mode, questioning with an obvious concern in her voice, "Okay, but what does that mean?"

Emily was doing her best to make it clear this was a sign from God, showing us His will and that she was *supposed* to go on this trip. God had a plan for her! After Emily finished speaking, Gloria simply smiled at the two of us and said, "Okay."

She handed us the necessary paperwork and payment, walked back over to her vehicle, picked up her bags, kissed her husband goodbye, and hopped right onto the bus. Emily and I exchanged a quick look of relief. We were amazed by what had just happened. We thanked God for helping us provide Gloria with what she needed to hear.

Later on, during our ride to Ohio, I went to sit with Gloria to tell her that I had the utmost confidence there was something absolutely beautiful waiting for her at this healing service. Because of this fact, perhaps the evil one had been trying to play tricks on her, causing her to doubt and question her original decision. "Fear is never from God," I told her.

I knew that if Emily and I hadn't been given these signs to help Gloria trust that she was doing the right thing, she would have gone back home that morning. She gave a huge sigh of relief, informing me how she had been praying specifically for signs from God with roses and knew she had been given an answer to her prayers. She thanked both Emily and me for sharing what we did and stated that was all she needed to hear. Happily, after this conversation, she was at peace with her decision to come on the trip.

We weren't the only ones being given signs. In addition to Emily, there were a couple more college students on the bus. One student, in particular, had traveled a long distance to be with us because she had been given her own signs that she was supposed to join this trip. One of these signs had come from her social media. Our Facebook posts for this healing service had come across her newsfeed several different times.

She knew God was calling her to join us when she realized there was virtually no other explanation as to how she would have found out about us. She is from a town that is located well over two and half hours away from where we were, we had no Facebook friends in common, and she didn't know anyone else on our trip. I laughed when she shared this strange coincidence. God had been relentless and kept calling her until she signed up.

She was a brave young lady, as her mother was supposed to have come with us, but then something abruptly had come up at the last minute, and her mom was unable to join her. This delightful, red-haired girl named Courtney knew she was to come with us no matter what, even though she didn't know a single soul. She seemed so courageous to me. I spoke with her mom briefly on the phone before we left, letting her know that we would take good care of her daughter. I could sense the concern in her voice, but she also knew it was meant to be. As a result, she trusted God had a plan and encouraged her daughter to make the trip.

During our journey to Ohio, we were all amazed at the politeness of our bus driver, Michael. He was an exceptionally nice guy who was a complete gentleman. We had pleasant bus drivers each time, but this guy seemed special. He displayed a caring nature. One of the ladies on our trip named Kim had her foot in an aircast boot and had to use a knee scooter for mobility. Michael had to load and unload this scooter with each stop. This was one of the many courtesies he extended to us. I knew this was a regular duty that came with his job, but even so, he seemed to work with his whole heart and always wore a smile. He was truly kind, and his presence really added value to our days.

Kim was another person I had taken notice of quite often in church. She was hard to miss. She would sit in a pew up front in church, having her scooter parked up next to her so that she would only have to take a step or two to reach it. Ever since we had first begun attending mass at Immaculate Conception in March, she had been in this boot. One evening in October, at the end of a church function, I had approached her out of curiosity as to why she had been in this situation for so long. I had never spoken to her before, nor did I know anything about her.

She told me she had broken a tiny bone in her left foot, the fifth metatarsal to be exact. It had happened back in February 2019 when she had been on a pilgrimage to the Holy Land. This stress fracture had occurred simply from constantly walking on the cobblestone brick roads and uneven pavement throughout Israel, which had taken a toll on everyone's feet and ankles. I was startled at how long it was taking for this bone to heal. I told her it worried me because it seemed excessively long. I can only imagine how many times she had heard that statement or thought the same thing herself.

She revealed to me that she had an autoimmune disease called Rheumatoid Arthritis and was taking an autoimmune suppressive drug for treatment. It's possible this drug was preventing her bone from healing properly. I told her that I used to have a different autoimmune disease, lupus, for which I had been taking the exact same medication for many years.

I think she was quite surprised to learn that I no longer had lupus. Saying it in the past tense indicated I had been cured, even though there supposedly is no cure for lupus. I knew she had heard about our bus trips, but she told me she honestly had never given it much thought or looked into what it was about. I told her she explore the idea as we had one coming up soon, and we still had room if she was interested. I shared a brief version of my healing story and how it all started with a prayer by a man of deep faith, a Catholic doctor, who was well-known and highly sought after. She was very intrigued by the details I gave that evening and wanted to learn more.

Kim and I met up for coffee a few days later before our third trip was to leave. One of the first things she told me was had I not spoken to her that evening and extended that personal invitation to attend the healing service, she probably would have never checked into it on her own.

The two of us talked for over an hour in a local café. We had a lot in common, especially when it came to our health issues, fears, and frustrations. I provided a chronology of my life over the last year, and she seemed to be inspired by what had happened to me. I felt as if I had known her for years and could have spent the entire day talking with her. Two days after we spoke, she officially signed up to come with us. I was so glad that she did. I knew God's hand was in it because it wasn't within my character to just walk over to someone I didn't know and ask them about their medical issues. I am normally rather shy, and so here was another moment where God compelled me to do something I wouldn't normally do, using my compassion and concern for what Kim had been enduring for so long.

As we were traveling on our way to Ohio on this third trip, I made a brief announcement that Emily would be passing out our customary cinch bags that we typically hand out on each trip. It was full of prayers, holy oil, the itinerary, etc., but this time, we had placed one extra item inside that the previous trips did not contain. I asked everyone to pull this special item out of their bag.

It was a gift from Butch Milling. He had so kindly written out his healing testimony and the words he was inspired to say during our second trip. These were the same powerful words that had helped to change Butch's and Tom's thinking and facilitate a major healing in both of them.

We took Butch's write-up, and we added the quotes we found sprinkled throughout the book, *Miracles Every Day,* where Dr. Nemeh gives his advice on how people should approach the healing service and prepare themselves for the prayer. We printed out a copy for each person with one goal in mind – to help each person be in the right state of mind to surrender, receiving healing, and to better serve God by their life. Each person was left with plenty of time during our time travelling to Ohio to contemplate this information.

Romans 12:2 (NRSV)
Do not be conformed to this world, but be
transformed by the renewing of your minds,
so that you may discern what is the will of God–
what is good and acceptable and perfect.

nineteen.

Never Give up on Hope

WE ARRIVED SAFE AND sound to the hotel the night before the healing service. Before dawn, I was wide awake and God spoke to my heart to make a few important announcements to the group first thing in the morning. I quickly pulled out my phone in the dark and made some notes about the topics I was supposed to address on the bus ride over to the monastery.

A few hours later, everyone grabbed some breakfast and loaded the bus for our fifteen-minute ride from the hotel to the healing service. I said a quick prayer, took a deep breath, and grabbed the microphone. I started with saying, "Good Morning! I wanted to take a moment before we arrive at the healing service to make a few quick announcements."

I paused, and then continued, "I know that some of you are having doubts about the healing service, doubts that you could be healed from a quick prayer."

I spoke to them about the power that comes from everyone praying for each other with Dr. Nemeh. All of our prayers, united together, have much more potential than we can possibly imagine.

At this point, my emotions were getting the best of me. I hesitated, but pressed my way through saying, "Since having my own healing and *everything* I have seen and experienced myself, I've still had doubts once in a while come to me, trying to persuade me that this stuff wasn't real. That is evil not wanting us to believe in these holy moments. I have learned to call on my guardian angel for help. To some, it may sound funny, but believe me they are *real*, and they are there to help you. All you have to do is ask."

I ended by imploring, "Please, please pray for each other today. When you receive your prayer, everyone else will be praying for you. So please take the time to pray for others."

After I finished speaking, we pulled into the monastery parking lot. Kathy was outside waving at us as we pulled up, and both she and the bus driver helped everyone off the bus. We invited the bus driver to come in and receive a prayer as well. He had been silently listening to all our stories over the past twenty-four hours on the bus and in the hotel. Surprisingly, he said that he was interested in doing so and agreed to come in and join us.

Emily and I were so happy to see everyone and ran over to hug Kathy and the doctor, along with the many volunteers we recognized from our previous trips. I spotted Butch and Mary Lou giving hugs too. They had been with us from the very beginning and their role in these trips seemed to grow each time. This trip, it was even more evident because they had brought many of their loved ones, and Butch, by sharing his insight about the purpose behind his healing, was instrumental in helping others to fully benefit from the healing services.

As we made our way into the beautiful monastery, I noticed the healing service was set up in the main chapel, which the Benedictine Monks had generously offered for our use that day. Dr. and Kathy Nemeh smiled and warmly welcomed everyone into the chapel. I noticed how they always remain humble, relaxed, and worry-free in nature, which completely describes their approach to the healing services. To our surprise, they invited a guest, Dr. Jeff Rediger, to come speak with our group at the end of the service about his new book, *Cured: The Life-Changing Science of Spontaneous Healing*. In this book, he dedicated an entire chapter to Dr. Issam Nemeh and his work.

I was impressed this doctor would take the time to speak with us about what he had learned from watching Dr. Nemeh. Dr. Rediger, along with another doctor, Dr. Patricia Kaine, were both featured on *The Dr. Oz Show* in 2011. Dr. Kaine is one of the reasons why Dr. Nemeh received national attention. Her terminal case of Pulmonary Fibrosis, which damaged and scarred her lungs, just disappeared after receiving prayers from Dr. Nemeh. Dr. Rediger was sent in to debunk the claim that she had been miraculously cured, but instead, was won over by the scientific proof resulting from the power of prayer.

After Kathy presented the exciting news about Dr. Jeff Rediger, she invited one of their beloved volunteers, Jessica, to share her story with our group. This was the same Jessica who had helped me through the second healing service when I was overcome with grief and doubts after hearing the news of Dr. Nemeh's father passing. Jessica stepped up to the front of the room and graciously gave us a peek inside her private life by presenting her personal journey with Dr. Nemeh. She told us it all began with a miraculous healing from Multiple Sclerosis, a debilitating disease also known as MS. Through Dr. Nemeh's prayers to God, she had been healed of MS years ago. There were additional miracles that took place later on in the lives of her four children, who had also received prayers from Dr. Nemeh for various medical problems, one of them being a cleft palate. Due to the many healings that she and her children had received, she began to volunteer at the healing services. Jessica wanted to give back to God for the many blessings He had given her and her family through the Nemeh's ministry.

Jessica has a very charismatic personality. She has a way of lighting up a room with her sweet spirit and smile. Following Jessica's testimony, Kathy Nemeh returned to the front and lovingly introduced her husband. She first spoke about a couple of patients who had recently seen her husband in the office. These particular patients each had cancer and had come to them as a last resort. I couldn't help but notice her timing in speaking about this topic as we had several different people on this trip who had been recently diagnosed with stage four cancer. Kathy told us about the various physicians who had told these same cancer patients that there was no hope.

Kathy became obviously agitated and expressed her disappointment in the medical field as a whole. She told us that no one should say such bleak comments to the people who needed words of encouragement the most.

She criticized their remarks saying, "How dare they say such a thing to someone! There is *always* hope. Hope is what we have to hold on to."

She told us how many of these same patients had received a prayer from her husband, and instead of passing away as other doctors had predicted, they got better. Some were one hundred percent cancer-free and living a normal and fruitful life. Kathy pleaded, "Never give up hope."

After she introduced her husband, Dr. Nemeh, he began with a short talk about faith. He spoke about how God is really moving and trying to get people's attention in the times we live in now. He said the proof of this is the growing number of people receiving healings over the years. He insisted, "The number of healings is going through the roof! God is *trying* to grab our attention."

Once he had finished speaking, Dr. Nemeh began praying over everyone individually just like he had done in the past. As people were being prayed over by Dr. Nemeh, it was evident that everyone was united together through prayer. Some were raising and extending their hands, joining in petitions from where they were sitting, and others were closing their eyes as they murmured their own heartfelt prayers, fixing them on whoever stood before Dr. Nemeh.

When Dr. Nemeh approached Kim, her foot was still inside the aircast boot. The doctor had asked her to remain seated. All at once, Kim started chuckling, and began exclaiming that there was a strange sensation taking place in her foot. She laughed again and said that she could feel the bones in her foot moving, and it felt like the doctor was moving them. She kept repeating how strange it was, since her foot was still in the boot. Dr.

Nemeh also laughed, and with a smile attested, "I am not touching your foot."

Throughout the day, we witnessed many others in the group, along with Kim, receive a healing touch from the Lord. Several people fell in the Spirit, and almost everyone experienced or observed the miraculous, such as bones moving back into place, nerves regenerating, scoliosis being reversed, and even cancer being taken away.

At the end of the day, Dr. Nemeh prayed over our large envelope full of photos and petitions. In this instance, Dr. Nemeh kept Emily sitting down in her chair and stood next to her as he held out his hand in prayer. The Holy Spirit flowed over the photos and over Emily, causing her to fall in the Spirit with her head gently leaning back as she rested her body against the back of the chair.

I placed my hand behind her head to help hold it up, however the weight of her head lying back was rather heavy. Art, the man I had met at the meeting in Cedar Rapids, sat directly behind Emily and assisted me with holding up her head. After a few moments, we also asked my son Josh for help too. The love of God pouring down from Heaven over all the people represented in photographs and petitions was so powerful that it once again had a strong effect on Emily.

After this beautiful display of God's love, Kathy Nemeh stood up and asked if anyone wanted to share what they had experienced during their prayers. There were a few moments of silence, and then a kind-hearted lady named Mary bravely spoke up to describe her encounter. She indicated that she had been unable to lift her arm before we arrived, due to a bad tear in her rotator cuff, which needed surgery. She further explained that after Dr. Nemeh had prayed over her, she felt great! In order to demonstrate her healing, she lifted her arm high above her head and beamed with joy. We all clapped to express our happiness for her and our gratitude to God.

After Mary got the ball rolling, many more people volunteered to share their story. The last person to speak up was Art, which surprised me because he was often reserved and quiet. He had a beautiful smile, and his eyes filled with tears while gazing at everyone around the room. He began saying, "Many years ago, my mother was very sick and dying. I know what kind of pain she was in and what kind of terrible things she had been through in her life. So, I asked God to give me all of her emotional pain and let her die in peace."

He paused, wiped away his tears, and continued in a soft voice, "God answered my prayer. I have been carrying around this pain since that day, and I could never let it go because I made a promise. But when Dr. Nemeh and all of you prayed for me, I felt it leave. For the first time in twenty years, this pain that I have been carrying left! I now feel the love and peace of God in my heart."

As Art expressed his sincere gratitude towards God, the Nemehs, and my family for this entire day and experience, everyone was moved by his incredible healing story from deep emotional pain. There was not a dry eye in the room by the time he finished speaking. It was a perfect ending to a perfect day.

As we prepared to leave, our group gathered in the entryway of the building to talk a little longer with Dr. Rediger, Dr. Nemeh, Kathy Nemeh, and the volunteers. Many people asked Kathy and the doctor if they would ever come to Iowa, appealing to them about the number of people who needed healing there and had heard about them, but weren't able to travel to Ohio with us for one reason or another. Kathy asked the doctor what he thought and they both agreed to start looking into planning a healing service in Cedar Rapids, Iowa. Everyone was elated at the thought of them coming out our way.

Before long, it was time for us to leave. Emily and I said our goodbyes to the volunteers first. We hugged them and expressed our hope to see them again sometime soon. Then we made our way over to Dr. and Kathy Nemeh. Emily and I were already tearful, and I could tell it was a tough moment for them too. Kathy sincerely requested that both Emily and I leave quickly before she started to cry. It was too late for Emily who was wiping tears away, and I was painfully aware that no matter how hard I tried to hide it, my sadness would still be written all over my face. Nevertheless, we each gave them one last hug before we finally slipped out the door and stepped onto the bus. Everyone waved as we pulled out of the drive.

When we arrived back at the hotel for our final night's stay, we gathered in a hospitality room and talked about the day. We arranged our chairs in a large circle to encompass everyone and to allow people to share their encounters. Some had experienced intense heat, bright colors, interior movement, bright lights, and some even said they visibly saw Jesus standing alongside Dr. Nemeh as he prayed over people. Many seemed to want to talk all night long as they were still wired with excitement from the healing service.

Nearly everyone joined us for the 8:00 a.m. Mass at a Catholic Church near Westlake, Ohio, the next morning before our departure back home to Iowa. I was astonished by the timing of the Gospel reading that day.

Gospel Reading on October 13, 2019:

Luke 17:11-19 (NRSV)

Jesus Cleanses Ten Lepers

On the way to Jerusalem Jesus was going through the region between Samaria and Galilee. As he entered a village, ten lepers approached him. Keeping their distance, they called out, saying, "Jesus, Master, have mercy on us!" When he saw them, he said to them, "Go and show yourselves to the priests." And as they went, they were made clean. Then one of them, when he saw that he was healed, turned back, praising God with a loud voice. He prostrated himself at Jesus' feet and thanked him. And he was a Samaritan. Then Jesus asked, "Were not ten made clean? But the other nine, where are they? Was none of them found to return and give praise to God except this foreigner?" Then he said to him, "Get up and go on your way; your faith has made you well."

During our journey home, I made a quick announcement about the remarkable timing of the Gospel reading at church. I said, "Everything happens for a reason, and the reading today was meant to remind us to never stop giving thanks or telling people about our healings. Christ actually invites us to share our healings so that others can come to believe in the power of God, or maybe even in Christ Himself, through our own stories. When we return back home, make a personal goal to share your healing with at least one person. It could change their life."

Following my statement, a lady on the bus who has helped me spread the word about the trips from the very beginning motioned for me to come sit by her because she wanted to ask a question about the healing service. She inquired that while she heard people say they felt healings happening inside them, she wanted to know why Kim wasn't able to just throw off her boot and start walking around, or why another younger gentleman, who was in terrible pain and had a cane to help him walk, wasn't all at once shouting he was pain free. She wanted to know why everyone didn't have an immediate healing right then and there.

I prayerfully thought about her question before I spoke. I told her there were several reasons why I didn't think it worked that way. First, there are the occasions where God does work swiftly, but most often, the work God does is not "showy," but rather is gentle in nature. I explained how my own healing took many weeks, and perhaps several months to fully manifest.

Second, I believe Christ does this to constantly call our mind back to Him. Each day we reexamine what changes have taken place and doing so causes us to be mindful of the beautiful work He is doing inside us. If I had had an instantaneous healing, my thoughts would not have been in constant union with His. I would have had my healing, been thankful, and perhaps just moved on with my life. God has a purpose for everything and gives us exactly what we need when we need it.

Then this lady told me that she didn't feel much during her prayer and wondered if anything would come about or not. I suggested she give it some time because God could very well be working in a similar, tender way with her physical injury, especially since these healings are usually progressive in nature, in order to draw our mind back to His. A few weeks later, this lady, along with the other two people she asked about, received beautiful healings, and they are included at the end of this book.

As the drive continued, everyone was so joy-filled that it made the time it took to travel 590 miles back home go by *almost* unnoticed. Once we arrived safely, we said our bitter-sweet goodbyes to people who had once been strangers and now were some of our closest friends. Some people exchanged phone numbers to stay in touch, and others exchanged hugs. It was an amazing and powerful weekend bound together with the Love of Christ.

Colossians 3:12-14 (NRSV)
As God's chosen ones, holy and beloved, clothe yourselves with
compassion, kindness, humility, meekness, and patience. Bear with
one another and, if anyone has a complaint against another, forgive
each other; just as the Lord has forgiven you, so you also must
forgive. Above all, clothe yourselves with love, which binds
everything together in perfect harmony.

twenty.

Art of Love

ON MONDAY MORNING, THE day after we arrived home from Ohio, I lay wide awake in bed and reminisced about the whole weekend. God never ceases to amaze me, especially during healing services, because His presence and healing touch are felt by each person in special ways. After my family and I had been prayed over by Dr. Nemeh that Saturday, I replayed my own encounter over and over in my mind while I gazed up at the ceiling.

When Dr. Nemeh approached me at the monastery, he didn't ask any questions or say much. He simply offered his kind smile and went straight into calling on the Holy Spirit. I closed my eyes and heard Kathy's words come up again in my thoughts. Kathy always tells us to come up for prayer with "faith, hope, and courage," and then she adds that the secret ingredient to this therapeutic recipe is "love."

As Dr. Nemeh began praying, I immediately began to think of my family. I thought of my husband Randy and then each one of my children. As their faces came to my mind, one at a time, I thought about how much I loved them as a form of prayer. I felt Jesus grow nearer to me in this moment, and I felt His love. Then I heard Dr. Nemeh softly whisper the word, "yes."

A few seconds later, I felt a tingling, vibrating sensation in my lower back. Then suddenly, I felt an intense heat in the same area, similar to what I had felt in my heart back in 2011. After I fell in the Spirit, I heard the doctor's footsteps as he walked away from me to pray over my daughter.

I stayed in the Spirit, sitting in my chair for a few minutes until the heat and tingling had ceased. I stood up and headed back to my original seat wondering what that was all about. I didn't have any time to really think about it until being back home.

While I reflected on this moment, I wondered what had been wrong with my lower back before the healing service. After a few minutes, I remembered how I had experienced pain in my lower back each time I would stand up from kneeling in prayer. I never thought much about it, nor did I ever wonder how or why it happened. I just knew the amount of pain I experienced was always directly related to the amount of time I spent on my knees.

I just attributed it to getting older, and I never paid much attention to it. Now I knew that when I felt heat and tingling in my back, God was healing me. At once, I hopped out of bed to test it out. I knelt beside my bed and prayed the rosary. When I finished, I stood up, and waited for the pain to hit. It never came...and it has never returned since.

Praying on my knees helps me focus on my prayers and connect more deeply with God. This healing was such an amazing blessing because it enabled me to pray on my knees for longer periods of time and grow closer to Him. Now every time I kneel in prayer, I bless His name and give Him thanks for this miracle and grace.

Not a day went by that I didn't think about the healing services, the new friendships that had blessed our lives, and God's wonderous ways. I continued attending daily Mass and compiling a list of healing stories from people willing to share them with me. Kathy and I also worked together to find ways to bring a healing service to the Cedar Rapids area.

Several months later, in late January 2020, I decided to stay after Mass to both thank God for His many blessings and to ask for His guidance in planning the future healing service in Iowa. I was on my knees with my head bowed in prayer for some time. When my eyes opened, I looked up and saw a lady sitting in the pew directly ahead of mine patiently waiting to speak with me after I finished praying. I sat back in my pew and realized I recognized her from church, but I didn't really know her very well.

We exchanged smiles and she asked if I remembered a gentleman named Art. She mentioned someone had told her that he was on our third bus trip with us. I said, "Oh yes. I know exactly who you are talking about."

She informed me that she had just heard he was recently diagnosed with stage IV pancreatic cancer. My heart immediately sank, and my mind began to race. I had trouble comprehending her words. I thought, *how can this possibly be? He was just prayed over.* I took a moment to process this information and return my gaze towards her. When I did, she proceeded to let me know that he was in hospice.

She paused for a second time, waiting patiently for me to process what she was saying. Each time, she simply gave me a loving smile as she waited for me.

I finally spoke, giving reasons for my confusion, "I am sorry. I just had no idea he was ill in this kind of a way."

I paused and then said, "He had a huge emotional healing when he came with us."

She nodded and told me she had heard that too and knew all about it. With kindness in her eyes, she reached for my hand and said, "I just thought you would want to know."

I nodded in agreement and asked if people could visit him. She thought that shouldn't be a problem, but she wasn't exactly sure which hospice it was. She thought maybe it was located somewhere near a street named Blairs Ferry Road in Cedar Rapids.

I thanked her for informing me and bolted out of the church trying to not cry as I ran to my car. I didn't know if I should go visit him or what I should do. I started crying as soon as I opened my car door. *Would he even want to see me?* I wondered. *It's so sad that he went to a healing service with us and found out, just three months later, he was dying.*

I cried out to God asking him for guidance on what I should do, as I laid my head down on the steering wheel. I pleaded out loud, "God, if you want me to go there and see Art today, you will have to show me the way as I have no idea where he is."

I started my car and began to drive towards the interstate. I drove a few miles and took the exit for Blairs Ferry Road. As I traveled down the exit ramp, I tried to discern, *which way should I go? Do I turn left...or turn right?*

Then I realized I could not think on my own. I needed to completely surrender and let God guide me, and without a single thought more, all of a sudden, my car shifted into the left turn lane. I sat at a red light waiting to make the turn and announced, "Jesus, I trust in You." When the light turned green, I made the left turn and headed west on Blairs Ferry Road. I was a little familiar with this road because of common grocery stores, but I never knew there was a hospice.

Just then, my cell phone rang. The call was coming from a dear friend of mine, Marilyn. I wasn't sure if I should take the call considering I was focused on God guiding me to the hospice house, but since I didn't know if she needed something important, I thought I had better answer.

As I talked with her, I was concentrating more on the conversation than my driving. I felt a nudge to turn off the road into a parking lot while I was on the phone. Taking notice it was a business parking lot I kept driving all the way through it, winding my way around the building almost like I knew where I was going, until I came across a small side road that led to another smaller parking lot. I pulled in and parked my car. As I continued listening to Marilyn, I glanced up for a second just to see where I was. When I looked above me, I saw the sign "Mercy Hospice."

I was astounded. I knew Marilyn's phone call was perfect timing because it allowed my mind to free itself from trying to decide where to go and increased my dependence on the Holy Spirit. I quickly told Marilyn something had come up and I had to go, and we hung up.

I sat there in awe, thanking God, but realized I still had no idea if this was even the correct place. I wondered what I would do or say if it was. I had never been inside a hospice, nor had I ever visited someone in this state before. I implored God to continue guiding me through this.

As I stepped inside, there was a volunteer who greeted me at the door. She looked up the name I gave her, confirming that Art was a patient there, and she checked in with his nurse to be sure it was okay to visit him. Once we had permission, we began to walk to the far side of the building together in silence. I was astonished at how peaceful and even beautiful it was there. As we approached his room, I could see that the door was closed. The volunteer knocked on the door, and we heard a man's voice softly say, "Come in."

The volunteer gave a tender smile as she turned to walk away. I slowly opened the door and shut it quietly behind me.

I peered around the corner of the room and saw Art lying in the bed on his left side, facing the opposite direction. The television was off, and the room was silent. I began to softly step through the room. At this point, Art was still unable to see who had come in through the door.

When I made my way around his bed, he lifted up his head to see who was there. I stopped moving when his eyes met mine. Everything seemed to stand still as we stared at one another. Slowly, he started to smile, and he broke the silence by softly saying my name, "Christy," while reaching out his hand for mine.

I held his hand, stood next to his bed, and explained that I had just heard of his situation only a few minutes ago and came straight over. I asked if he was okay with my knowing about his condition and being there to visit him. He insisted he was by replying, "Absolutely! Thank you for coming."

I was still nervous what he thought about my being there, and I couldn't believe this was happening to him. I took things slow and allowed him to lead the discussion. He began by thanking me for handing him the information to the healing service and for providing him the opportunity to go. This was surely a comment I never saw coming.

He informed me how that one event back in October led him to begin having peace in his life again, which in turn, initiated a process of deep healing in all of his relationships. He told me that his reconciliation began with his adult children and continued with putting an end to some long-time quarrels with his siblings. He further explained that after the healing service and into the month of November, many of his relationships that had once been severed by past mistakes and misunderstandings had become fully restored. He attributed everything as a direct result of the miraculous emotional healing he had experienced at the service in October. Art continued to share that many of these relationships had been strained throughout most of his life and were entirely healed in only one month's time.

Then, I asked him when he found out that he was sick. He told me that the doctors didn't know exactly what was wrong until December 21.

At that time, they not only diagnosed him with stage IV pancreatic cancer but also notified him the cancer had metastasized to his liver and was inoperable. As he was speaking, I could no longer hold back my tears. I kept wiping them away, and when he noticed my sorrow, he focused his eyes intently on me and claimed, "I am not sad. I am ready to go whenever God calls me. I am at peace."

He continued and mentioned that the healings with his loved ones were essential for him. It helped give him the peace he needed to get through his diagnosis and the fact that he didn't have much time left on this earth. He said the invitation to the healing service was when the first steps to forgiveness and renewal began. We spoke for a little while longer, but then I could tell he needed some rest.

As I was preparing to leave, he reached out for me to take his hand again. When I did, Art lovingly commended my daughter and me for following God's will in our lives. Then, he said, "I think that in allowing God to work through you, you are taking Jesus by the hand and are lovingly bringing him to others."

His kind words touched my heart so deeply that I was weeping as we hugged in parting. As I said goodbye to Art, I whispered, "Goodbye for now, my dear friend…until we see each other again."

Art Petrzelka, at the age of 67, passed away on March 22, 2020.

Art's story taught me a huge lesson about God's Healing Touch. God heals us in ways that we may not expect, but He *always* gives us exactly what we need when we need it. Art's healing helped him pass from this life into the next in peace and love. The love of his family and friends were all brought back to life again before God called him home.

God's Love for us *is* the reason behind the miracles. With great love and mercy, God uses miracles to wake us up and restore our relationship with Him before He calls us home. Dr. and Kathy Nemeh have opened my eyes to this truth as I have witnessed their love for everyone and everything around them. As children of God, we are all called on this journey...to Love.

Matthew 22:36-38 (NRSV)

"Teacher, which commandment in the law is the greatest?"
He said to him, "'You shall love the Lord your God with all your
heart, and with all your soul, and with all your mind.' This is the
greatest and first commandment.

twenty-one.

Healing Stories

MIRACLES HAVE A WAY of awakening our minds to the fact that with God, all things truly are possible. Each one of these stories was given to me personally from the person who had either experienced a healing from one of our bus trips or had observed a healing in the life of a loved one whose photo or prayer petition had been in the large envelope prayed over by Dr. Nemeh. Either way, these stories are completely authentic and directly state what happened to individuals after they received a prayer from Dr. Issam Nemeh.

The testimonials in this chapter are only a select few from the many I have learned about and collected over the last year. I am not able to incorporate all of the astounding miracles that have been shared with me due to private/personal healing stories and the fact that I don't want to exhaust this meaningful content. However, I am delighted to present these incredible stories from the people we have met and come to love in this past year, as God's unfailing love for us is reflected in each of them.

Healings from In-Person Prayers:

I was blessed with several healings...

My eustachian tube was healed and I could finally hear clearer; my rotator cuff was torn and the healing took this pain away; my low back scoliosis pain has improved tremendously along with a displaced tailbone and I feel taller, walk straighter, and the heavy weight and constriction I felt before is gone.

It was such a wonderful spiritual experience to witness the healing of others as well as my own. Dr Nemeh is so kind and gentle. He and his wife Kathy are very special, and they share this gift of healing with everyone!

†   *-Mary V.*

As Dr. Nemeh approached me, he asked what my health issues were. I told him I had a broken bone in my left foot (fifth metatarsal) that was very slow to heal (four months and counting, I told him). I told him I've had rheumatoid arthritis for almost forty years, and I had spondylolisthesis (Spondylolisthesis is a slipping of vertebra that occurs, in most cases, at the base of the spine). I told him the problem was the fourth and fifth vertebra (L4 & L5). Dr. Nemeh knew exactly what and where it was.

He began praying over my foot first. After a while, I felt movement INSIDE my left foot, totally independent of Dr. Nemeh, who was not touching it! This felt weird, but amazing - - like jello! There was definitely something happening there. Dr. Nemeh also worked on my spine, this time touching and manipulating it, while bending me backwards. He felt the vertebrae moving and indicated healing took place. I started crying midway through, while repeating "Thank you, Jesus."

That evening, my foot was noticeably swollen and red and a little warm to the touch. I thought that was odd and even a step backwards, but then when I shared this with Christy and Emily the next morning (and showed them photos), they said it seemed like this was a sign that the blood was flowing, that healing was progressing, and that, sometimes after a healing, you go through some pain, sickness, or odd feelings for a while as the healing progresses.

Regarding my back/spine, Christy noticed I walked/moved a little faster after the healing session, especially down the bus steps, indicating the probability that my back was indeed healed. In addition, a friend (who didn't go on the trip) mentioned she thought my back looked straighter, or it looked like I was standing up straighter! One of the symptoms of spondylolisthesis for me was after bending over, I felt excruciating pain when trying to straighten back up and had to do so very slowly. After Dr. Nemeh's prayer, I was able to bend over and stand back up straight without any pain whatsoever, almost as if the vertebra had gone back to their original locations!

Regarding my foot, the day before our trip, I got an x-ray, which showed improved, but not total, healing. My next appointment with my podiatrist is November 14, at which time he will take another x-ray. My foot, in general, already feels better (and is not as swollen as the night of the healing session), but it's hard to tell what condition it's in when I've been wearing this boot for four to five months. The x-ray will be proof. I praise God for loving me so much, touching me so intimately, and bringing about the healing I needed (in whatever form it ends up being). Who knows what else has been "healed" in me, whether it is physical, spiritual, emotional, etc.? I continue to trust in Jesus. I am thankful for the opportunity to meet Dr. and Kathy Nemeh -- and for this incredible experience!

†   -Kim S.

Dr. Nemeh asked me what I needed healing for. I told him about my metastatic breast cancer, and where it is located. He extended his hands over the areas, and it felt very warm in those areas. He was praying quietly the entire time.

Then I mentioned lifelong pain in the low back. He lightly touched the area I mentioned. Dr. Nemeh said, "You had an injury from a fall, a very bad injury."

This was absolutely true. I fell on my tailbone back in my early teen years and have had intermittent pain since then. Then he asked, "Can you feel that?"

I could feel my tailbone moving. Through the Holy Spirit, that old injury from thirty-five years ago, was fixed. I can tell that the bone is sitting at a different angle. The pain has gradually decreased.

After working on my tailbone area, he went back to the areas with cancer and prayed some more. After he was done, he asked if I am taking vitamin D. I said I was and told him the dosage. He told me to take five times the amount I was already taking. I trust him, so I have increased the dose, to the level he recommended.

I had two mouth sores at the time, which is a common side effect from one of the medications I am taking. The next morning, I noticed that they were completely healed.

I do not know if I experienced full healing of the cancer, but my trip to see Dr Nemeh began a healing journey including the healing of body, mind, and soul. I am not the same person I was before I went to see him. I do not know where the future holds, but I am excited to see where God leads me next!"

†   *-Julie S.*

**UPDATE - *I, the author, personally ran into Julie's father at a church function a several weeks later, who said she had a new scan performed and had received the new results just a day ago.*

He proceeded to tell me that Julie originally had cancer in several lymph nodes, three spots in the bone, and several spots in the pleura (the sac-like structure containing the lungs). Julie had two more recent scans, one that showed some very minor improvement before attending, and another scan that was done a few weeks after the bus trip to showing moderate improvement in all areas.

The new scan detected no cancer in the bone, cancer in only one lymph node, and a considerable decrease in size of the masses in the pleura. Six months later after this scan another one showed further decrease in size of the remaining cancerous lymph node. One mass in the pleura has disappeared completely. There is still one mass in the pleura, but it has continued to shrink in size.

Before the trip to see Dr. Nemeh, I had been diagnosed with Stage IV prostate cancer. My odds weren't good of survival rate.

With surgery, the doctors were saying I had less than a 12% chance of survival.

However, since our trip to Ohio with the prayer service, I had my prostate removed and a few of my lymph nodes for testing. To the doctor's surprise, and my own as well, the cancer was not nearly as bad as originally thought and previously diagnosed.

The doctors are now giving me a survival rate of 91%. Thank you, Jesus!

† -Larry L.

**UPDATE - Larry updated us in February of 2020 that his two latest prostate-specific antigen (PSA) tests came back negative. He is now completely cancer free.

The Holy Spirit definitely came upon me. I still feel the peace and best of all, peace of mind. I am sleeping wonderfully, and I am not worrying. I still have a lot of restored energy. My heart feels more loving.

Also, there was a sore muscle that I didn't tell him about. He put his hand on my sore shoulder muscle from a fall a few days prior, I felt a warmth from Dr Nemeh's hand and the muscle was immediately better. He also knew which vertebrae occasionally goes out without me showing him. I went to reach around to show him and he already had his finger on the exact vertebrae that I had injured back in the 80's.

It is hard to pray in the desert. I seem to have found an oasis this past weekend.

✝ *–Diana*

Mary says the pain in her right shoulder is gone. Her neck pain is much better, and her hearing has improved.

I have noticed a change in the feelings in my legs and my back. I have been pain-free in both since the healing service. The biggest change for me was from the shoulders on up – in my mind and thoughts. I had a stroke awhile back and have been left unable to even read a book since. However, since the healing service, this ability has been fully restored. I have in the last two months read two books from cover to cover. For the first time in years, I have been able to read.

Thank You! God Bless

✝ *–Leon and Mary H.*

Dr. Nemeh stood in front of me and asked what I needed healed. I told him I have numbness and fatigue in my arms and legs. He then proceeded to pray over me while touching my back and neck. I was slain in Spirit where I saw a white light and fell back into my chair unable to physically move. I felt a strong tingling sensation down both arms. The feeling began to go away and then Dr. Nemeh prayed over my legs while touching my knees. I immediately realized that I no longer had numbness in my arms.

Later in the day, Dr. Nemeh was finishing healing a few other people in my group and I kept getting a voice in my head to ask Dr. Nemeh to come look at my legs again. I did not feel comfortable doing such a thing when there were many other people present who were much worse than me, so I finally told the voice, "If you want him over here, you ask him."

I full heartedly believe this voice was the Holy Spirit because a few moments later, Dr. Nemeh came over to me and asked to pray over my legs again. I felt a stronger healing sensation down my legs this time. Dr. Nemeh told me it may take a few days before my legs will be healed. I am still waiting and praying for my legs to be healed since I saw Dr. Nemeh only three days ago but I have faith that the Holy Spirit works miracles through Dr. Nemeh.

 †   -Courtney C.

It is hard to put into words all the grace filled moments. When Dr. Nemeh prayed over me I felt such peace and love. It was like Jesus was right there and I did not want to leave.

I realized on the bus that I could turn my head all the way to the left without any pain. I truly know I had a healing there.

†   -Kathy S.

I have kidney cancer. I have had one kidney removed and now cancer is in the remaining kidney. I went into this whole event skeptical and almost changed my mind last second and didn't go, but somehow, I got through those doubts and went on the healing service trip.

When Dr. Nemeh came up to me and asked me what he could do for me I told him about my cancer but I asked if I could possibly stand in for others that I know who also have cancer, thinking there wasn't much he could do for me? He smiled and began praying. I can't say that I felt any sensations at the moment of the prayer.

The next day however our group went to mass together and that morning I had a sense of peace come over me that washed away all my emotional baggage I have been carrying around for over twenty years. I have continued to carry this peace with me since that day.

I am not sure yet if I had a physical healing, although people have been telling me and noticing that I have, since the prayer, received a pinkish color back to my face.

I am so thankful for Dr. Nemeh and for coming on this trip. The peace I have now with whatever happens is worth more than I can possibly say in words.

†   *–Mike S.*

UPDATE – *Mike had a CT scan a few months after the healing service in October. There was no growth since the prior scan. Then nearly six months later, which made it almost eight months since the healing service, Mike had another CT scan preformed and received the best news! His cancer had completely disappeared, even all the spots in his lungs. He was now one hundred percent cancer free! Please be mindful that this all happened* **without *any treatment! He was not undergoing chemo or radiation.*

After looking at the new scan, the doctor told Mike that he would not have known Mike had ever had cancer if he didn't personally know his past history.

Before the healing service began, we were encouraged to pray for one another as Dr. Nemeh prayed over each person. There is such power in praying for one another.

(James 5:16)-Pray for one another, that you may be healed.

As Dr. Nemeh was praying over people, I could feel the Holy Spirit at work. I could see Jesus in my spirit walking among us praying and healing and touching us.

When my turn came to be prayed over, I was asked to stand up and Dr. Nemeh asked me what he could do for me. I mentioned a couple of things and then said I surrender everything to Jesus. Within a short time, I was resting in the Spirit as I fell back, someone helped me to sit in the chair. While I was resting in the Spirit, I had a tremendous PEACE come over me. It was a peace that I felt I wanted to stay there forever. As I was sitting there, God gave me a vision of beautiful colors, pastel colors (pink, blue, purple, etc.) I looked and looked as it seemed like a long time at these beautiful colors, swirling together back and forth covering the entire area of my vision, so beautiful.

Then came the vision of my family. We have three children and ten grandchildren. They were lined up in three rows, starting with our oldest son, his wife, and their two children. Then our second son, his wife, and their three children. Then our daughter, her husband, and their five children. This went on for some time. I don't know for sure what this vision meant, but I am guessing that Jesus was showing me He has them in His hand protecting them and healing them as well. He knows how I have been praying for them and their salvation. I had a tremendous peace come over me again. I didn't want to leave this state of mind I was in. Thank you, Jesus, - Praise you Lord.

We have such an awesome God, who loves us so much. We are His children and He wants nothing but the best for each of us. He needs our "Yes" to serve Him and to follow Him. Our reward is waiting for us in Heaven.

Pray, trust and don't worry.

†   -Mary Lou M.

I find it very difficult to find the words to express what I saw and experienced during our healing service with Dr Nemeh. I took my son, Adam, who suffers with a spinal cord condition, which caused permanent damage in his legs, making it extremely difficult for him to walk. This condition caused him a lot of pain and was progressively getting worse over time. It's been very difficult to watch my son suffer over the years and fearing that it would be only a matter of time before he would not be able to walk any longer and end up in a wheelchair the rest of his life.

By the grace of God, my son received healing. His pain is completely gone, and his legs no longer shake when he gets up to walk. He's doing things he hasn't been able to do for years and was told he will continue to heal as time goes by. Praise God! The extreme gratitude and thanksgiving I feel is beyond words! There is nothing more painful than a mother watching her child suffer, so, I also received healing when my son was healed.

Many of our group experienced healings and there was such joy and love felt by all; I didn't want this time together to end. Dr Nemeh takes no credit for these healings, he told us all to give thanks to God, which I have over and over again, but I also am thankful to Dr. Nemeh for saying yes to God's plan to use him in such a powerful way to help so many people. I pray God blesses him abundantly.

I promised God if he would heal my son, I would shout his love and goodness from the roof tops and do my best to bring hope to others by believing in his healing power. I pray I can live up to that promise.

   †   *-Sandy K.*

I was skeptical about going to the healing service. I went to it with an open mind and it was a wonderful experience. I have a cyst on my spinal cord resulting in bad nerve damage putting me in excruciating pain. During the healing service, I felt a presence that I feel was Jesus entering my body when Dr. Nemeh was praying over me. He told me I was getting a healing, but it would be progressive. It's been five days since I've seen Dr. Nemeh.

I have a neuro stimulator in my back to trick the pain receptors in my brain and I've had it shut off since the day I seen Dr. Nemeh. I'm pain free in I don't know how long, and my walking and balance are getting better day by day.

Thank you!

† *-Adam K.*

Healings from Photo/Petition Prayers:

A friend of mine had a severe stroke and couldn't even bring himself to go back to work for years. A week or so after the healing service in October where his picture was prayed over, all at once, I heard he went back to work, after several years of no improvement.

† *-Submitted by Diana*

My sister had been very sick with a cold for two weeks. There was no medicine that helped whatsoever. She had plans to leave on vacation soon. The morning after the prayers over the picture by Dr. Nemeh, she woke up and was completely well, all signs of the illness were instantly gone! She was able to keep her travel plans and go on vacation as planned.

† *-Submitted by Mary V.*

Our granddaughter moved far away from our family with a person who was not good for her and was living in a sinful relationship. She had been gone for years with not much communication or hope in sight. A few days after Dr. Nemeh's prayer for her, she simply got up, and moved back home while breaking off the relationship.

†   *-Submitted by Anonymous*

Our daughter had been relocated for work and had to move far away. She was trying to sell her house for months, against all odds, since it was located on a street block with all brand-new construction homes for sale. She had been managing two mortgages and her stress level was quite large. Two days after the healing service, she had a buyer and her house was officially sold.

†   *-Submitted by Anonymous*

My son had been battling severe depression and had attempted suicide. After receiving the prayer, he was a brand-new person, willing to go out and participate more in life without any medication or doctor's intervention. This seemed to come out of nowhere, but we know where it came from. It came from God.

†   *-Submitted by Anonymous*

Our daughter was in a bad relationship for years. The guy was almost to the point of being abusive to her. We had prayed for years for her to leave but she wouldn't. He wouldn't even work to help support her and her children. The day after the service he upped and left her out of the blue. We are so thankful!

     †   *-Submitted by Anonymous*

My relationship with my spouse had been at all-time low. I had his picture in the envelope as he wouldn't come with me, while I was there also to receive a prayer for healing. Since the trip we have found common ground and it seems to be a completely new marriage. It has been wonderful!

     †   *-Submitted by Anonymous*

My aunt had recently informed us that she had been sick for some time. The doctors said she had cancer, telling her to prepare for the worst. I placed her picture in the envelope in the October healing service for a prayer, without her knowing anything about it.

A short time later, I received a phone call that something miraculous had happened right after the healing service. She said she was in a deep, peaceful sleep and woke up in the middle of the night completely drenched in sweat from head to toe. She had an awareness deep inside her that God had healed her that night. I told her about the picture I brought for a prayer and she had no doubt it was from this act that she received a healing.

A few weeks later, she went in for a checkup. To the astonishment of her doctor, all her bloodwork came back completely normal. Although my aunt was not surprised at all, the doctor could not understand it. My aunt told her doctor what happened, but they didn't believe it was possible. They had her come back another time to retest everything...and again, all results were perfectly normal, as if she had never been sick.

Thanks be to God!

† *-Submitted by Christy B.*

A relative had been seeing different doctors for fifteen years with no definite answer to the cause of her seizures. Three days after the healing service, she was referred to a new specialist, AND she received a diagnosis for the seizures, which resulted in finally locating and being prescribed medication!

† *-Submitted by Mary V.*

A relative had triple bypass surgery six months prior, went in for six-month post-surgery checkup, given one month to increase heart function by two percent or would need a pacemaker. Had appointment for tests two days after the picture was prayed over at the healing service, heart function had increased by six percent. So, no pacemaker!

† *-Submitted by Mary V.*

My husband and I met a couple named Tom and Joan a few years ago when Tom came to the hospital where I work to have radiation treatments for his lung cancer that had metastasized. We realized that we all belonged to the same church and quickly became friends. Over the past three years, I've wondered why God brought Tom and Joan into our lives, as they are a bit older than us and are currently in their 80s - perhaps Dr. Nemeh is part of the answer.

I went on the July 2019 bus trip to a healing service in Ohio with Dr. Nemeh. We knew Tom couldn't make the trip, but he and his wife understood that God can work miracles whenever he wants and were willing to send a picture of Tom with me to be prayed over after the service. Unfortunately, the healing didn't come through at that time for Tom.

As the months went by, Tom's condition continued to worsen. He was taking both chemotherapy and radiation treatments. Little by little, he was losing his strength and energy. Since the fall of 2019, he had become so bad he would hardly move from sitting on the sofa. His body continued to become more swollen, and his pain level was increasing. His legs became so enlarged and painful that he referred to them as big tree stumps. He was getting to the point of hardly eating, drinking, or even moving.

In spring of 2020, Tom's oncologist was nearing the point of sending him home to die. Tom's pain increased with each passing week. He was hospitalized for three days in June 2020. While in the hospital, Tom's oncologist and cardiologist visited him at the same time.

Tom's wife Joan sent out an email updating me saying, "Tom's oncologist said that with Tom's body condition and having tried so many different chemos for lung cancer for five years, there just wasn't any more treatment he could give Tom. Chemo is hard on the whole body, especially the heart. Tom's whole lower body had become swollen; basically, from his chest all the way down. The nurse told me that you normally don't see that much swelling."

Joan continued telling me that all four of Tom's heart valves were not working. The cardiologist said his heart was now at a 40% efficiency. Both specialists agreed that since there was nothing more they could offer to fight the cancer or help his heart, it was time for Tom and Joan to call upon hospice for help. In our area, patients are given the option of hospice when they have a terminal diagnosis while having a prognosis of less than six months to live.

A few weeks later, we were able to bring Tom to a Dr. Nemeh "virtual" healing service in Cedar Rapids. We remained in Iowa as Dr. and Kathy Nemeh stayed in Ohio. We had to bring Tom in a wheelchair because of his weakening condition.

During the prayer, Tom didn't feel much, but he said there was definitely a brief time during the prayer when his pain was completely gone, a rare moment. Also, during the prayer, Dr. Nemeh said he could feel Tom's heart doing something which we took to mean healing!

It has been six weeks since Dr. Nemeh prayed for Tom's healing via Skype, and the difference in Tom is amazing! He has been "claiming" his healing by regularly thanking God for it. He is eating again, and his energy has come back! His tree-stump legs are back to normal size and are just about pain-free. The difference in him is undeniable!

Three weeks after the service, I asked Tom how he would explain such an incredible improvement. His wife, Joan answered, "Dr. Nemeh," while simultaneously Tom replied, "The Good Lord."

Tom later said, "With God anything is possible!"

† *-Submitted by Jean B.*

Psalm 147:3 (NRSV)
He heals the brokenhearted, and binds up their wounds.

twenty-two.

The Miracle of a New Life

THE PICTURE OF KATIE Schultes that we took with us to the October 2019 healing service.

During Katie's first trimester of her pregnancy, she bled profusely several times. The first time at the ER she was told she had a large tear in her placenta and to go home and wait, that the baby may or may not be fine.

The next time she bled heavily, her doctor told her the tear had gotten even bigger, and to go home and wait.

The third time of heavy bleeding took her back to the ER again, and she was again told to go home and wait. This brought her up to about her 15th or 16th week of pregnancy.

That's when we told her about Dr. Nemeh and sent a photo to Christy and Emily to take of her holding her hands in the shape of a heart over her growing womb. (She wasn't supposed to try to attempt the bus trip in light of the recurring bleeding episodes.)

Over the weekend of the healing service in October, while Katie was NOT along on the trip, she will tell you she was "in tune" with what God was doing in her life. It was a special weekend for her in several ways. Then, at her next regular checkup, the doctor couldn't find the tear in her placenta!

Here's what Katie texted to me after seeing the doctor:

> *'Guess what!?!? My obstetrician said she's fascinated by my case and my ultrasound today. She had a hard time finding any source of bleeding from my placenta, even though those tears do not heal themselves. She said she didn't expect me to carry this baby a long time after*

seeing the initial bleed/tear in early September. Baby looks great and is growing like a weed. OB feeling very hopeful. This is NOT a coincidence!'

Katie said it was as if her very experienced doctor was trying to convince herself there was some explanation for the missing placental tear. The doctor was searching for it with the ultrasound and talking aloud to herself but couldn't talk herself into any scientific explanation for the tear to be gone!

Katie knew in her heart the truth. She was elated!

There was no more bleeding during the rest of her pregnancy, and baby Summer Anne arrived on Friday, February 28, 2020 as healthy as can be!

Thanks be to God!

And to His good servant, Dr. Nemeh who prayed over Katie's picture with faith - - a faith that heals.

† *-Submitted by Jean B.*

**UPDATE - *I, the author, spoke with Katie on the phone about her story after the birth of her beautiful daughter, and Katie gave me some additional details to add to her story.*

Katie said, "The obstetrician (OB) mentioned she had been practicing for thirty years, and never had she seen a subchorionic hemorrhage as large as mine. In most cases with much smaller hemorrhages, the outcome still was not good. My OB told me when she had originally seen the tear, she wasn't hopeful at all, and she never expected me to carry beyond twenty weeks into the pregnancy. She now calls me her "miracle patient."'

Photograph of Katie Schultes & Baby Summer Anne

.

The miracle that Katie received from God echoed throughout the miraculous birth of her beautiful baby, Summer Anne. This beautiful testimonial is only a glimpse into the never-ending story of God's love for all of us.

Psalm 30:2 (NRSV)
O LORD my God, I cried to You for help, and You have healed me.

This book was written entirely for the Glory of God.

a picture is worth a thousand words,
but memories are priceless

THIS IS A SKETCH of Dr. Issam Nemeh drawn by my daughter, Emily Blake, at the age of thirteen. The first time we met the doctor in 2011 must have made quite an impact on her as she drew this one year later. Emily had tucked it away and forgotten all about it until we accidentally stumbled on her drawing when I was in the process of compiling the miracle stories. It was such a wonderful surprise, and I thought it would be a lovely addition to this book.

Psalm 143:5 (NRSV)
I remember the days of old,
I think about all your deeds,
I meditate on the works of your hands.

acknowledgements.

S INCE THIS BOOK IS about how my life changed to serve God and to help others through my own healing and spiritual journey, all of which took place due to Dr. Issam and Kathy Nemeh following God's plan for their own lives, my first acknowledgement goes to the two of them.

I have the deepest amount of respect, admiration, and love for these two people and their entire family. They have taught me how to serve and love everyone, which has helped shape me into who I am today. They are my biggest role models, and Kathy Nemeh is one of my closest and dearest friends. If it weren't for the two of them following where Christ has led them, I most definitely would not be where I am today.

The second acknowledgment I wish to make is to my daughter Emily. She has been on this spiritual journey with me from the beginning and has seen all the highs and lows. The highs are when we are closest to Jesus and see Him in everyone and in everything, and our hearts are lit with the fire of our love for Him. When my lows hit, she is the one who helps keep my feet planted on the straight path and reminds me to trust Jesus always, no matter what is happening around me.

Emily helps me to see all the beautiful blessings surrounding us and to understand why we are in this role together. She knows the love I feel for each person I meet and the fire I feel in my heart for Christ, and she understands how I live each day entirely for God. She knows, feels, and understands because everything that has happened to me spiritually has happened to her as well. She is my confidant, and I am beyond blessed to have her on this journey with me.

My heart overflows with gratitude for my husband, Randy and my children – Collette, Josh, and Matt – who have watched both Emily and me go from living "normal" Christian lives to presently living our faith to the extreme, where our every step, breath, and heartbeat is fully lived for God first and everyone else second. They have each had to go through this process and growth with us in a sense. Although they didn't necessarily understand what they were witnessing, they have always supported and loved us through all the changes. This whole process has most definitely opened my eyes to how big of a heart my husband truly has. I love you so, Randy.

I owe a huge thank you to Kim Smith, who was on our third trip with us to Ohio. Once she heard I was writing a book, she very generously offered to help with the editing process. I can only imagine the patience this must have taken with a first-time author. Thank you again, Kim, for all you have done, and most of all for your friendship. You are a treasure to me more than you will ever know.

My heart goes out to all the people who went with us on these bus trips to Ohio, some of whom are now some of our most cherished friends. I thank you for trusting and following where our Lord led you. I truly love each and every one of you! I wish to also express how much I appreciate everyone who submitted their testimonials to make this book come to life and to help others believe in the power of God...today.

My last thank you is one that is eternal. I thank God for everything, as EVERYTHING is a gift from Him.

1 Peter 4:10-11 (NRSV)

Like good stewards of the manifold grace of God, serve one another with whatever gift each of you has received. Whoever speaks must do so as one speaking the very words of God; whoever serves must do so with the strength that God supplies, so that God may be glorified in all things through Jesus Christ. To Him belong the glory and the power forever and ever. Amen.

about the author.

Christine M. Blake and her daughter Emily
had tremendous healings on all levels in January 2019. These amazing
transformations were primarily due to the prayers and faith from Dr.
Issam Nemeh. Since that time, Christine and her daughter Emily
have dedicated their lives to helping others learn about Dr. Issam and
Kathy Nemeh and the ways our Lord is still walking and healing us
today.

More information can be found about Christy & Emily by going
to their website:
www.theblessedreasontrip.com

_____

To learn more about Dr. Issam Nemeh visit:
www.pathtofaith.com

Made in USA - Kendallville, IN
1183091_9781735533292
10.20.2020 0947